A Child's First Library of Learning

Simple Experiments

TIME-LIFE BOOKS • ALEXANDRIA, VIRGINIA

Contents

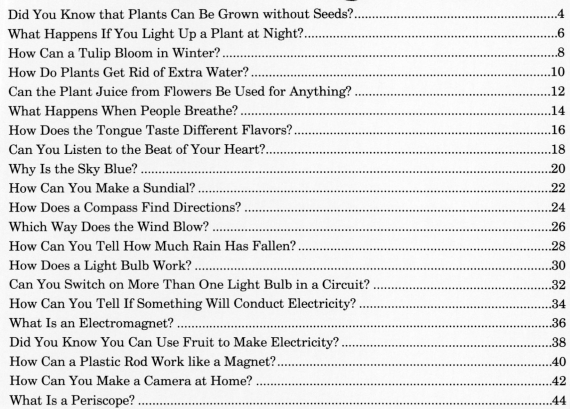

? Did You Know that Plants Can Be Grown without Seeds?

ANSWER Most plants grow by sprouting from seeds or bulbs. But some plants will grow from a leaf, or a shoot, or a piece of the root that is stuck in the ground. Others produce buds at the tips of their leaves or along their stems. When one of these buds is put into soil, it will grow into a new plant.

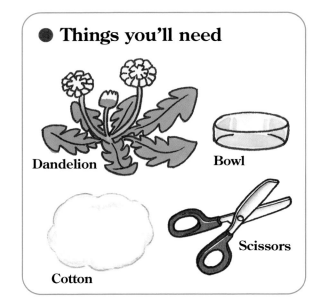

● **Things you'll need**

Dandelion

Bowl

Cotton

Scissors

■ Plants from roots

Dig up a dandelion root. The root is long and does not break easily. If you replant it, even if you have only a part of it, the root will sprout a new plant.

▲ If you keep the cotton moist, the root pieces will sprout leaves in two to three weeks.

▲ Fill a shallow bowl with wet cotton, and place the root pieces on it.

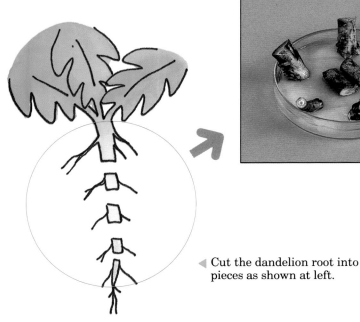

◀ Cut the dandelion root into pieces as shown at left.

■ Plants from leaves

A single leaf from some plants will put down roots and become a new plant when placed in soil. In the experiment at right, the leaf of a mum with a tiny bud near its stem is used. Plants with thick, fleshy leaves, like the sansevieria shown below, right, need only a part of the leaf to make a new plant.

▲ **Mum**

▲ **Leaf with a bud**

▲ **Plant the leaf**

▲ **Leaf sections**

▲ **Each section sprouts**

▲ **Sansevieria**

■ Grafting plants

Grafting is a method of joining parts of two related plants to make a new plant that combines the best qualities of the two. Often the stronger plant serves as a base. Part or all of the weaker plant is grafted onto the rooted stronger plant. The rooted plant is cut straight across and notched with a V-shaped groove. A section of the weaker plant is put into the groove, and the two parts are held together with string or tape. The cut section of the rooted plant should be at least 2 inches above ground.

● To the Parent

To every gardener's despair, dandelion roots sprout easily, no matter how damaged they are. Many plants can grow from just a root or root section. Others, such as mums, begonias, and African violets, can sprout from a leaf. Some bushes and trees develop from a single branch planted in the ground. Grafting is more difficult because the cut surfaces must be arranged so that the water- and nutrient-carrying vessels of the two plants will connect.

❓ What Happens If You Light Up a Plant at Night?

ANSWER Most flowers open and close in response to light. If you take a plant that blooms only early in the day—a morning glory, for example—you can fool it into blooming at a different time by giving it more light at night and less in the daytime.

● **Things you'll need**

Potted morning glory

100-watt light bulb

■ Turn night into day

Plant a morning glory seed in a small pot. When your plant is about to flower, you can experiment. Normally morning glories open by 6 a.m. Keeping the plant in the dark until 7 a.m. and making its day longer by shining a light on it from dusk until midnight will change the plant's pattern. It will bloom at noon instead of morning.

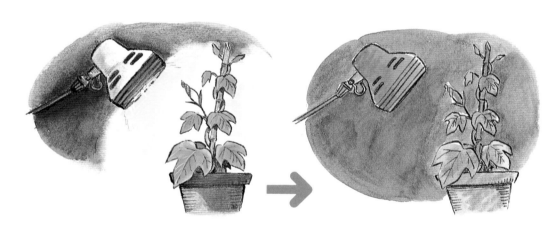

▲ Place the light about 3 feet from the plant, and let it shine from dusk until midnight for about a week. You can use a lamp timer to turn the light on and off at precisely the same time each day.

▲ At midnight turn the light off and make sure that the room is totally dark.

■ Nature's way

In July, a morning glory that is growing outdoors will open its blossoms early in the morning. By noon the flowers will be closed again.

▲ **2 a.m.**

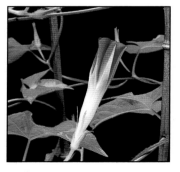

▲ **4 a.m.**

▲ **6 a.m.**

■ Hothouse mums

Mums usually bloom in the fall. Their normal blooming time can be changed in greenhouses by lighting them at night as if it were daytime and controlling the temperature.

▲ At 7 a.m. let sunlight into the room. In the outdoors the sun would be up much earlier.

▲ The morning glory will open fully by about noon.

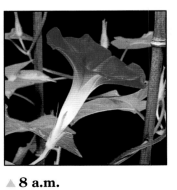

▲ 8 a.m.

▲ 9 a.m.

▲ 11 a.m.

How Can a Tulip Bloom in Winter?

(ANSWER) When winter turns to spring, tulips begin to bloom in the garden. But tulips can bloom much earlier. The bulbs must first be chilled to winter temperatures, then taken into a warm room to make them sense spring weather. Properly planted, the bulbs will begin to sprout when it is still winter outdoors.

Flowers in winter

● **Things you'll need**

Bulbs   Flowerpot

▼ After tulips have finished blooming in the garden, dig them up. Let them dry, and store them in a cool, dark place.

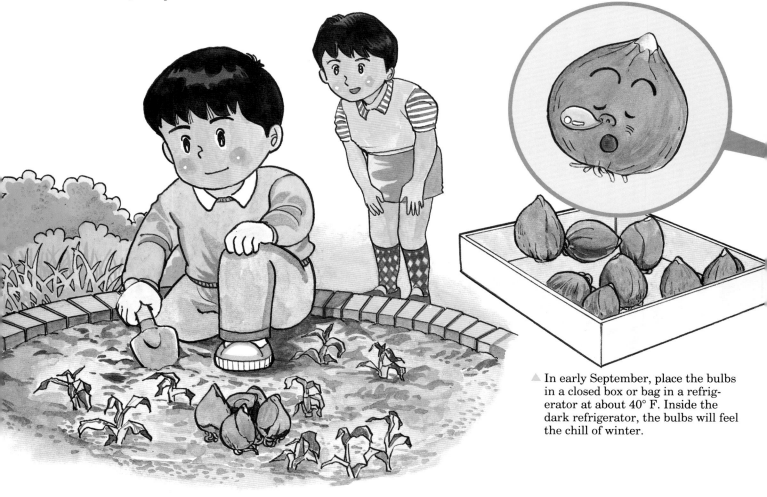

▲ In early September, place the bulbs in a closed box or bag in a refrigerator at about 40° F. Inside the dark refrigerator, the bulbs will feel the chill of winter.

You can experiment with different bulbs. Plants that can be forced into early bloom include the narcissus, hyacinth, and crocus.

▲ Hyacinth

▲ Crocus

◀ Plant the bulbs in a pot in mid-December. Keep the pot in a cool place indoors (about 55° to 65° F.) until the first sprout appears.

● **To the Parent**

Forcing bulbs to bloom is called low-temperature conditioning. Bulbs need about 12 weeks of cold-weather simulation before they can be brought out to be potted. The soil should be kept moist, but not soggy. If you do not mind having pots with soil in the refrigerator, you can plant the bulbs right away. When the shoots are approximately 5 inches tall, move the plants to a warm, sunny location. It will take between three and five weeks for the plants to begin to bloom.

❓ How Do Plants Get Rid of Extra Water?

ANSWER When people are hot, they sweat to lower their body temperature. Perspiration also rids the body of waste products. In a similar way, plants get rid of extra water they have absorbed. Water travels through the plant from the roots to the leaves. Any excess water is lost through pores in the plant's leaves. This process is called transpiration.

● **Things you'll need**

Plant

Plastic bag

Bottle

String

■ Transpiration

Dig up a plant—preferably a weed—with its roots, and place it in a bottle of water. Tie a plastic bag around it, and watch the bag cloud up with water from the plant's transpiration.

■ Where does the moisture come from?

Wrapping the plant in a bag in the first experiment proved that the plant transpires. Now cover different parts of the plant. Tie one bag around the stem and another one around a leaf, as shown at right, to see where the transpiration comes from. Tie the plastic tight so the water will not leak.

▲ Only a little water collects in the bag that is tied around the stem. The stem gives off barely any moisture.

▲ The bag tied around the leaf collects a lot of water. That shows that the leaves produce the transpiration.

❓ What's It Like inside a Leaf?

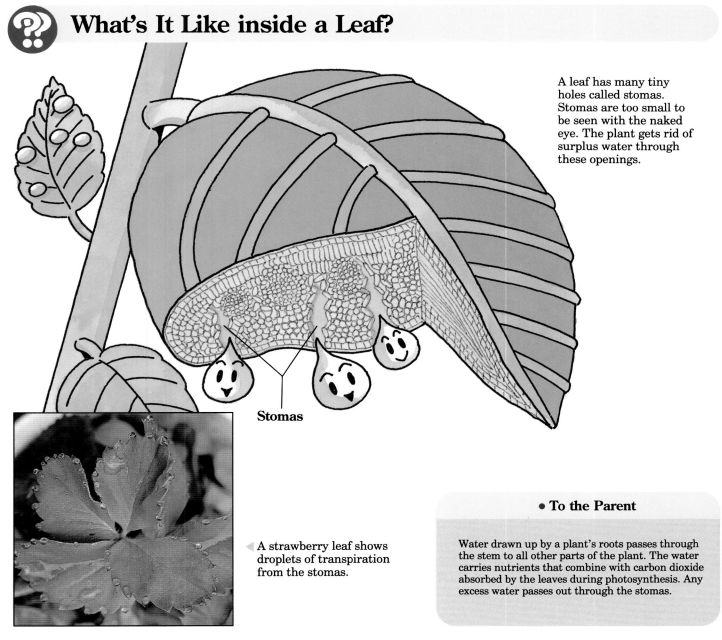

A leaf has many tiny holes called stomas. Stomas are too small to be seen with the naked eye. The plant gets rid of surplus water through these openings.

Stomas

◀ A strawberry leaf shows droplets of transpiration from the stomas.

Can the Plant Juice from Flowers Be Used for Anything?

ANSWER If you crush flowers of one color, from one type of plant, you will get a liquid of the same color as the flowers. This plant juice can be used to dye paper or fabric. But there are surprises: An orange flower may make a purple dye, or the juice from a violet flower can turn out to make yellow.

● Things you'll need

Flower

Mallet

Leaf

White fabric

Plastic bag

Construction paper

Scissors

Posterboard

Vinegar

Gauze

Cup

■ Patterns from leaves

▲ Position the leaf

You can imprint the pattern of a leaf on paper. Fold a piece of construction paper, and place a fresh leaf inside. Gently tap the leaf with a wooden mallet until the outline of the leaf appears.

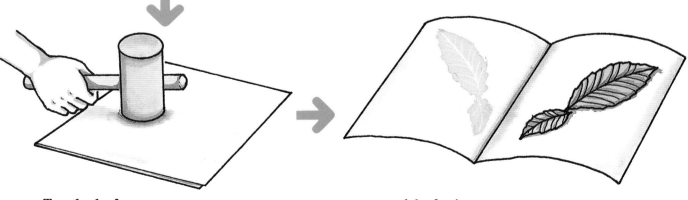

▲ Tap the leaf

▲ A leaf print

■ Dye experiments

Put flowers of one color into a plastic bag. Add a few drops of water. Knead the bag until you have plant juice. Drain the juice into a cup. You can use it like paint.

If you take the plant juice from a blue flower and add some vinegar to it, the liquid will turn red.

■ Dyes made from plants

▲ Wrap flowers in gauze and knead.

▲ Cut a design in a piece of posterboard.

▲ Place the cutout over a white piece of fabric, and dab it with the dye bag.

▶ The shape of the cutout appears on the fabric.

● To the Parent

Dyeing fabric with natural dyes can be a lot of fun, although you should take precautions against staining. These dyes can be hard to remove. If you want to achieve a particular color scheme, test the plant juices first. Dahlias, for example, no matter what color they are, will always render yellow. Cotton and wool are easiest to dye. Fabrics of certain vegetable fibers like rayon or linen do not accept vegetable dyes readily, but they can be prepared with a fixative to absorb the dye satisfactorily.

What Happens When People Breathe?

ANSWER When people breathe, they take air into their lungs and push it out again. Breathing depends on the movement of the diaphragm, a dome-shaped group of muscles below the lungs. When these muscles contract, they enlarge the chest area, making the air pressure drop and the lungs take in air. When the diaphragm muscles relax, the chest gets smaller and air rushes out of the lungs.

● **Things you'll need**

Plastic bottle

2 balloons

Straw

Scissors

Modeling clay

Tape

■ A model of the lungs

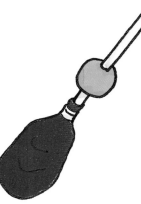

▲ Blow up one balloon to soften it. Tape this balloon to one end of the straw. Wrap modeling clay around the straw a few inches above the balloon.

▲ With the help of a parent, cut the plastic bottle in two along the dotted line as shown in the illustration.

▶ Place the straw in the bottle's neck and seal the opening with the clay. Cut the top off the second balloon, and stretch it over the bottom of the bottle.

How the lungs work

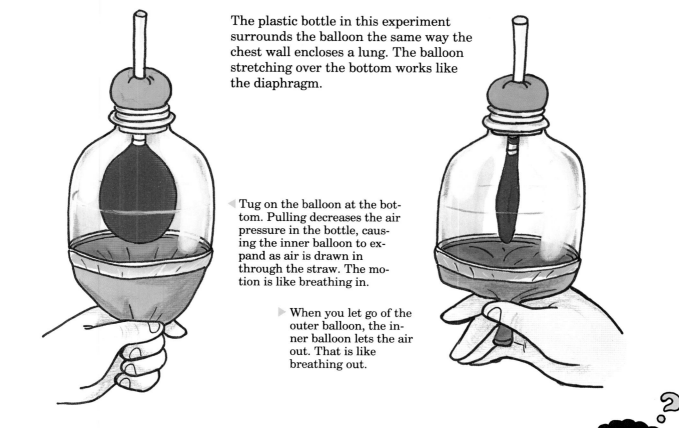

The plastic bottle in this experiment surrounds the balloon the same way the chest wall encloses a lung. The balloon stretching over the bottom works like the diaphragm.

◀ Tug on the balloon at the bottom. Pulling decreases the air pressure in the bottle, causing the inner balloon to expand as air is drawn in through the straw. The motion is like breathing in.

▶ When you let go of the outer balloon, the inner balloon lets the air out. That is like breathing out.

How lungs expand and contract

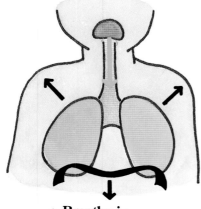

▲ Breathe in

▲ Breathe out

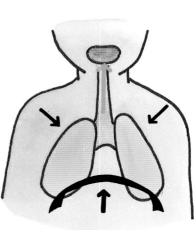

The balloon stretched across the bottom of the bottle is like your body's diaphragm. As it contracts and relaxes, the lungs breathe in and out.

● To the Parent

In this experiment the inner balloon moves like a lung, the balloon at the bottom like the diaphragm. If you pull the bottom balloon, the air pressure in the bottle drops and air flows through the straw, as if through the windpipe, causing the inner balloon to inflate. The same principles apply to the human body. When the diaphragm moves down, the size of the chest cavity expands and air pressure drops; air flows in through the windpipe, and the lungs expand.

How Does the Tongue Taste Different Flavors?

ANSWER The surface of the tongue is covered with tiny bumps called papillae. These bumps hold the taste buds that sense the four basic flavors: sweet, sour, salty, and bitter.

● Things you'll need

Cotton swabs

Salt

Sugar

Vinegar

Coffee

■ Try it

To see which part of the tongue is sensitive to which taste, put the four substances listed in separate cups. Dissolve the dry ingredients in water. Dip a cotton swab in each cup, and apply it to different sections of your tongue to find out where you taste flavors on your tongue.

▲ Sugar

▲ Salt

▲ Vinegar

▲ Coffee

▲ Tip of tongue

▲ Sides of tongue

▲ **Surface of tongue**

■ Results of the tests

With which part of your tongue could you taste the different flavors? Note where each taste was strongest, and compare that with the results in the circle at right.

The sense of smell also affects how things taste. Hold your nose while you eat a dough-nut. Does it taste as good?

The back of the tongue tastes bitter things.

The front sides and tip taste salty things.

The tongue's sides taste sour things.

The tip of the tongue tastes sweet things.

▲ **Tip and sides of tongue**   ▲ **Back of tongue**

● **To the Parent**

Tiny projections on the tongue, called papillae, contain the taste buds. These are assigned to specific tastes. The four basic tastes—sweet (sensed at the tip of the tongue), salty (at the tip and front sides), sour (at the center of the sides), and bitter (at the back)—combine to make up all flavors. In addition the smell, texture, and temperature of a food help to determine that food's flavor.

Can You Listen to the Beat of Your Heart?

ANSWER The heart never rests; it beats for a whole lifetime without stopping. You can feel your heart beating by placing a hand on the left side of your chest, especially after you have been running. If you use a doctor's stethoscope, you can actually hear your heart beating. To make your own version of a stethoscope, follow the steps below.

● **Things you'll need**

Rubber tube   **Funnel**

■ **Making a stethoscope**

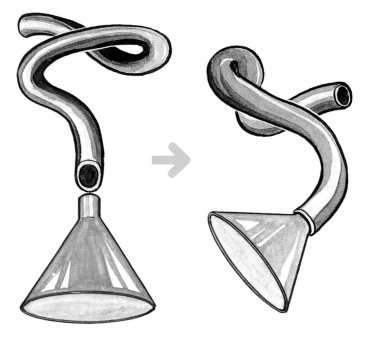

▲ Stick the funnel into one end of the rubber tube. Fasten the joint tightly with string or tape.

▲ Hold the loose end of the rubber tube to your ear. Do NOT stick it into your ear or you may damage an eardrum. Place the funnel on the left side of your chest. You will faintly hear the steady thump of your heart.

Why Can You Feel Your Heart Beating?

Each time the heart beats, you can feel the pulsing of an artery at the red points shown at right. Place a finger on any of these points so that you can feel the pulse.

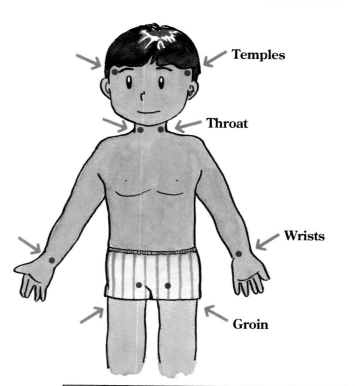

Temples

Throat

Wrists

Groin

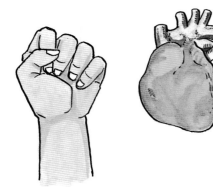

▲ Did you know that the heart, one of the most important organs in your body, is only the size of your fist?

■ How a stethoscope works

The metal disk picks up the sound of the heartbeat. The rubber tubes and earpieces carry the sound to the user's ears.

▲ Stethoscope

● To the Parent

The heart is the pump that regulates the body's circulatory system. Blood enters the heart's right upper chamber, or atrium, and passes into the right ventricle. From there the blood is pumped into the lungs, where it is refreshed with oxygen. The blood reenters the heart at the left atrium, passes into the left ventricle, and exits the heart through the aorta to circulate again. The contraction and expansion of the heart create the pulse rate.

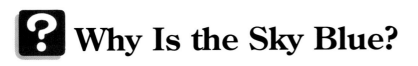

Why Is the Sky Blue?

(ANSWER) Sunlight looks white, but it contains all the colors of the rainbow. These colors move in waves of different lengths. Red, at one end of the color band, has longer wavelengths than blue, at the other end. Dust and water vapor scatter the short blue wavelengths more than the red ones. So, mostly blue light reaches the eye, and the sky looks blue.

● **Things you'll need**

Lamp

Fishtank

DRY MILK

Stirrer

Powdered milk

■ The colors of light

In the experiment below, a fishtank (or a glass baking dish) filled with water and a few spoonfuls of powdered milk represent earth's atmosphere.

◀ Fill the fishtank with water. Add 2 teaspoons of powdered milk per gallon of water. Stir the water to dissolve the milk.

▲ Shine a lamp (or a flashlight) on the end of the tank so that the beam of light goes through the liquid. If the light's path is not clearly visible, add another spoon of milk.

▲Darken the room and observe: From the side, the water looks bluish; from the end opposite the light, it looks reddish. This experiment shows the different paths of long and short wavelengths.

■ Why it looks blue

White light from the sun or a light bulb is a mixture of the colors of the rainbow. The particles of powdered milk in the tank scatter the blue, violet, and green parts of the light to the side; seen from that direction the water looks blue. The red, orange, and yellow parts stay at the center, making the light look reddish from the end of the tank.

How Can You Make a Sundial?

ANSWER A sundial is a simple clock, used since ancient times. You can still tell time with a sundial by seeing where the shadow of the pointer falls on a circle marked with the hours of the day.

● **Things you'll need**

Poster board

18″ dowel

Protractor

Scissors

Compass

Tape

■ Building a sundial

To make the dial, draw an 18-inch circle on a sheet of poster board. You can draw the circle with a pencil tied to a 9-inch-long string that is pinned to the center of the board. Mark the circle with 24 equal divisions for the hours.

1/4″

Fold

90°

Fold

9″

To make the pointer, or gnomon, draw a triangle on poster board, beginning with a 90° angle on top. Find your latitude on a map, or use the list on page 23. Mark the angle where the triangle meets the base *(marked with a star)* with the same degrees as your latitude. Add tabs and cut the triangle. Fold the tabs along the dotted lines, and attach the dowel with tape.

Back of dial.

Glue

Punch a hole in the center of the dial, and push the dowel through until the triangle sits flush against the dial.

Where do you live?

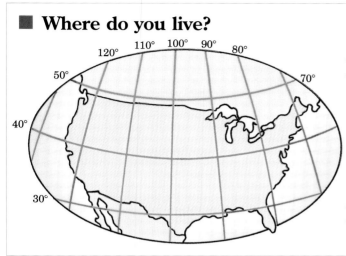

Anchorage, AK........61°
Atlanta, GA.............33°
Chicago, IL.............41°
Dallas, TX...............32°
Denver, CO.............39°
Honolulu, HI ....21°
Los Angeles, CA......34°
Miami, FL...............25°
Santa Fe, NM..........35°
Seattle, WA.............47°
Tucson, AZ ....32°
Washington, DC ......38°

The lines on this map of the United States show degrees of longitude and latitude. Longitude measures distances east and west; latitude measures north and south. First find the latitude of your city so that you can slant the sundial's pointer correctly. When you use this angle, the pointer's shadow will show the right hour.

Using the sundial

Place the sundial outdoors in a place where the sun can reach it all day long. The shadow line on the dial points to the hour of the day.

▲ Make sure the sundial rests on an even surface. It will not show the correct time if it is not level.

◄ With the help of a parent, use a compass to position the sundial so that the gnomon points south. During daylight saving time, the dial has to be turned by 15° to make up for the hour's difference.

? How Does a Compass Find Directions?

(ANSWER) A compass is an instrument that finds north and all other directions. The compass's magnetic needle lines up with the earth's magnetic field. When the needle stops spinning, it points to the magnetic north pole. Once you know where north is, you can find south, east, and west.

● Things you'll need

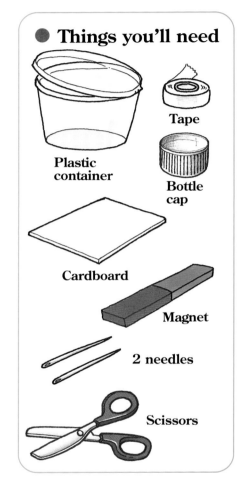

Plastic container

Tape

Bottle cap

Cardboard

Magnet

2 needles

Scissors

■ Making a compass

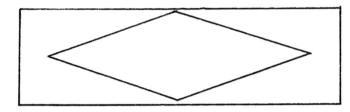

◀ Trace over the diamond shape at left, and cut the shape from cardboard. Color one half of the diamond red and the other half blue. This will be your compass needle.

▼ Rub a magnet about 30 times over both sewing needles, moving from eye to tip.

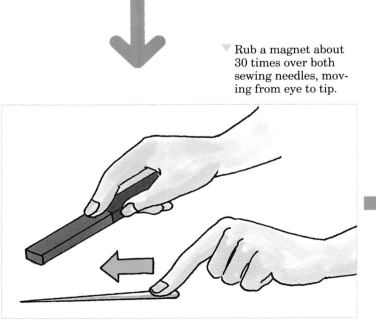

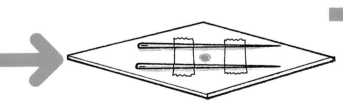

▲ Fasten the magnetized needles to the back of the diamond with tape. The red end should be over the needles' tips.

Orienteering

In orienteering, groups of people use a map and a compass to find their way through the woods. The team that finishes the course in the shortest time wins.

◀ Center the diamond shape, needles down, on the cap. Fasten the lid onto the container, and watch the needle spin. When the needle stops, the red tip will be pointing north.

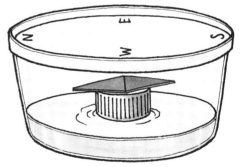

▲ Mark the lid where the needle points north with the letter N. At the blue tip, mark an S for south, an E for east, and W for west, as shown.

▲ Fill a clear plastic container half full of water. Float a plastic bottle cap, open end up, on top of the water.

● **To the Parent**

A compass helps you find directions because its magnetic needle is freely suspended in alignment with the earth's magnetic field. As long as the compass needle is not influenced by another magnet, it will always point north. The simple toy compass works well, but it will have to be remagnetized from time to time.

Which Way Does the Wind Blow?

ANSWER Weather vanes twirling atop roofs shift with the wind. A vane's arrow points in the direction from which the wind is blowing. If the wind is blowing from the north, for example, the arrow points north. You can make your own weather vane by following the steps below.

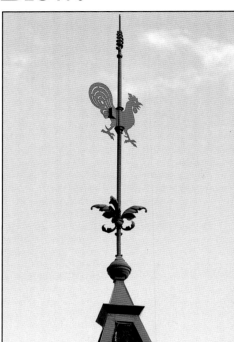

▶ Many weather vanes are shaped like animals. The rooster faces the direction the wind is coming from. A rooster-shaped vane is often called a weathercock.

■ Making a weather vane

Feather

Feather

▲ On a 2- by 3-inch rectangular piece of poster board, draw the outlines of two "feathers" and cut along the dotted lines.

▲ Glue the feathers to each side of the stick. The feathers will be pushed by the wind.

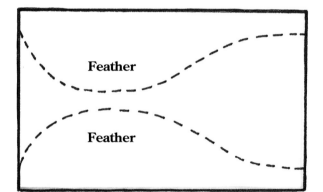

▲ Mark the center of the board with a cross, as shown. Place a square of plastic wrap on top.

▲ With the help of a grownup, cut a square notch in the plastic pipe so the stick will fit snugly into it. Find the center of the back of the board, and drive the nail through it. Fit the pipe over the protruding nail.

Things you'll need

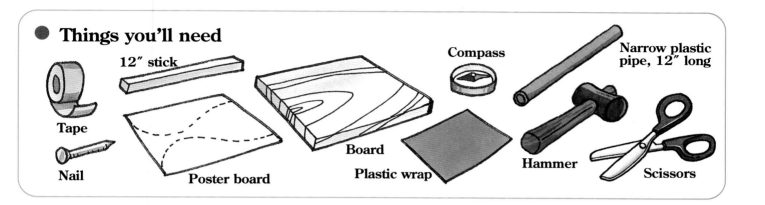

Tape

12″ stick

Nail

Poster board

Board

Compass

Plastic wrap

Narrow plastic pipe, 12″ long

Hammer

Scissors

Insert the stick into the pipe's notch, and wrap tape around the pointing end, or arrow, until the vane is balanced horizontally. If the stick fits too loosely, fasten it with glue or tape.

Set the weather vane outdoors in an area where the wind can hit it at full force. Place a compass next to your weather vane to find north *(pages 24-25)*. Mark the four sides of the board with the directions N, S, E, and W, as shown. Now you can tell which way the wind blows.

• To the Parent

Weather vanes are usually placed on top of spires and high rooftops so that the wind has access to them from all sides. For a backyard project, the weather vane should be as far as possible from tall buildings and other obstructions, because the wind changes direction around buildings.

How Can You Tell How Much Rain Has Fallen?

ANSWER Rainfall is measured by an instrument called a rain gauge. It shows how many inches of rain have fallen in an hour or in a day. You can build a rain gauge and measure rainfall for yourself. A simple gauge can be a straight-sided jar marked with fractions of an inch, similar to a measuring cup. Fit the jar with a funnel and place it securely in the ground to keep it from tipping over in a storm.

● **Things you'll need**

Glass jar

Can

Funnel

Indelible marker

Trowel

■ A simple rain gauge

With a ruler, mark a straight-sided jar with lines that show inches, half inches, and quarter inches. Or mark a strip of masking tape and stick it to the jar.

Place a funnel that is not much larger than the bottom of the jar into the mouth of the jar. The two should fit together without gaps.

■ Collecting rain

▲ Set the jar into a larger can. Bury the can nearly up to its rim to keep the gauge from overturning in stormy weather. Make sure that the rain can reach the gauge from all sides.

▲ Collect the rain for an hour or a day. The scale will show how many inches of rain fell. If you are collecting for more than a day, check the amount at the same time every day and write down the daily measurements. Then pour out the water and set up the gauge again.

● **To the Parent**

This experiment is useful during a season when it rains a lot. By keeping daily notes, your child will have a complete record of that period's rainfall. The more detailed the measuring scale is in fractions of an inch, the more accurate your child's records. Be sure to mark the scale using indelible ink.

How Does a Light Bulb Work?

ANSWER Every time you switch on a lamp, a stream of electrons travels through the cord to the light bulb. As the electrons jostle each other on their way, they create heat. This heat makes the wire, or filament, inside a light bulb glow. You can see how this works by building a simple light bulb that glows for a very short time.

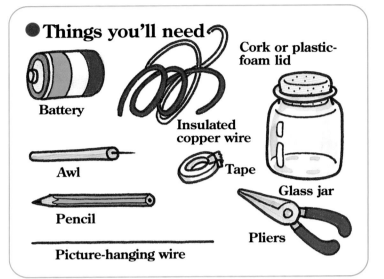

● **Things you'll need**

Battery

Insulated copper wire

Cork or plastic-foam lid

Awl

Tape

Glass jar

Pencil

Pliers

Picture-hanging wire

■ Making a light bulb

With the pliers, strip the insulation from both ends of two lengths of copper wire of different colors *(far right)*. Push the wires through the holes of the cork or plastic-foam lid.

▲ Separate the strands of the picture-hanging wire and wrap one strand tightly around the pencil. Slide the wire off the pencil. It now looks like a coiled spring; this is your filament. Attach the ends of the filament to the ends of the copper wire by twisting them together below the cork lid.

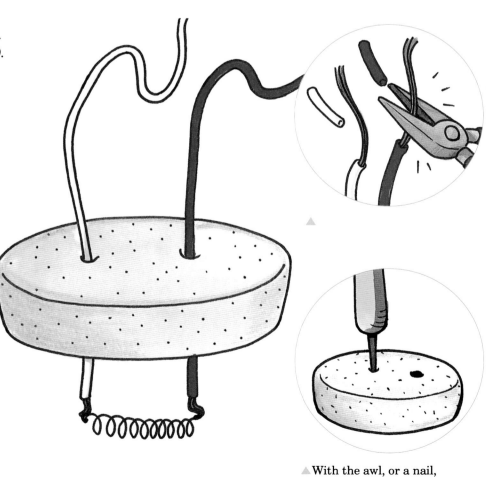

▲ With the awl, or a nail, punch two holes into the cork or plastic-foam lid.

30

The light bulb

Place the lid on the jar and press it down. Fasten one of the wires to one of the battery terminals with tape. Touch the second wire to the other terminal. As soon as you make the connection, the wire coil will glow dimly for a brief time.

Make sure that the copper wires and the picture-hanging wire are twisted together tightly or they will come loose when you put the lid on the jar. Darken the room. When you touch the loose wire to the battery, you will see the filament glow. CAUTION: DO NOT TOUCH THE WIRE COIL. IT WILL BE VERY HOT.

• To the Parent

An adult should supervise this experiment. Batteries that produce between 1½ and 12 volts are safe to use. But the filament wire can get red hot and will burn a child. Even before the wire glows, it will be too hot to touch. If the experiment does not work on the first attempt, try a shorter coil or wind the wire more tightly. If you increase the voltage by connecting two batteries or go to a 6-volt battery or higher, the light bulb will glow brighter but burn out faster.

❓ Can You Switch On More Than One Light Bulb in a Circuit?

ANSWER If you connect a flashlight bulb to a battery, the bulb will light. You can light more than one bulb from one battery in an arrangement called wiring in series. In another arrangement, you can also use more than one bulb by connecting each one separately to the same battery. This is called wiring in parallel.

■ A simple circuit

With the pliers, strip the insulation from the ends of the socket wires so the copper wires show. Screw a flashlight bulb into the socket, and tape the stripped wires to each end of the battery.

● Things you'll need

Bulbs Sockets Batteries

Tape Insulated copper wire Pliers

▶ When the wires are taped to different ends of the battery, the circuit is completed and the bulb lights up.

▲ If both socket wires are taped to the same end of the battery, the bulb will not light up.

▲ When only one wire is taped to the battery, the circuit is not completed and the bulb will not light up.

■ Lighting two bulbs

Wiring in series

▲ When two or more bulbs are connected in a line, they are in series. All the bulbs will glow, but because the electricity has to go through each bulb in turn, they light up dimly. If one bulb burns out, the whole string will fail.

▲ When two or more batteries are connected in a line, the arrangement is also called wiring in series. The more batteries you use, the brighter the bulbs will glow, because you are increasing the voltage.

Wiring in parallel

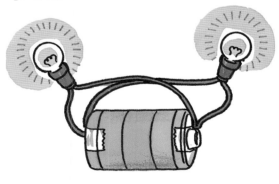

▲ When two or more bulbs are connected so that each is on its own complete circuit, they are wired in parallel. No matter how many bulbs you connect, the brightness of each will not change, but the battery will be used up more quickly. If one bulb burns out, the others will continue to glow.

▲ When two or more batteries are connected, the batteries will last longer than a single battery.

● To the Parent

When a light bulb is connected to a battery, the force with which the battery makes electricity flow, called voltage, sends electrons through the wire. The electrons move from the negative pole of the battery through the light bulb to the positive pole. That flow of electricity makes the bulb light up. When bulbs are connected in series, the electricity flows from one bulb to the next, with each bulb receiving less electricity than the one before. All the light bulbs light up but only dimly. When they are connected in parallel, they all get the same amount of electricity, rather than decreasing amounts, because the electricity travels separately to each bulb.

How Can You Tell If Something Will Conduct Electricity?

ANSWER There is a simple way to find out whether a material conducts electricity. It is done with an instrument called a circuit tester. You can build a circuit tester from a battery and a flashlight bulb. If you are testing a material that conducts electricity, the bulb will light up.

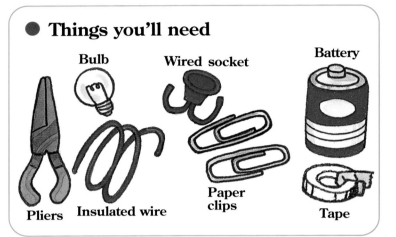

● **Things you'll need**

Bulb

Wired socket

Battery

Pliers   Insulated wire   Paper clips   Tape

◀ When a light bulb lights up, electricity is flowing along a wire through the socket into the bulb's filament and out again.

■ A circuit tester

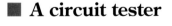

3 Strip the insulation from both ends of a piece of wire. Twist one end around another paper clip and tape the other end to the bottom, or negative end (–), of the battery.

2 Tape the end of one socket wire to the top of the battery, or positive end (+), and twist the end of the other wire around a paper clip.

1 With the pliers, strip the insulation from the ends of the socket wires so that the bare copper wire shows.

34

■ Testing objects

With your new circuit tester, you can test any material to see if it will conduct electricity by touching it with both paper clips. Among the objects shown here, only the aluminum can and the pencil lead conduct electricity. Try the circuit tester on wood, a book, or any other material in your house.

▲ Glass

▲ Modeling clay

▲ Pencil lead

▲ Aluminum can

▲ Book

■ A test with water

Touch the circuit tester to water in a glass. Then add a teaspoonful of salt to the water and test it again. Ordinary water *(below, right)* does not conduct electricity, but salt water *(below, left)* does.

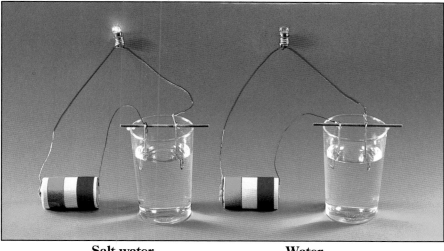

Salt water   **Water**

● To the Parent

Metals and some other materials have "free electrons" that easily escape from individual atoms and move within matter. Free electrons have a negative charge. When you touch metal with a circuit tester, the electrons move toward the positive terminal through the bulb and cause it to light up. Solutions, such as salt water, that have charged particles called ions will also conduct electricity.

? What Is an Electromagnet?

ANSWER An electromagnet is a magnet that attracts iron when electricity passes through it. Unlike a permanent magnet, an electromagnet does not attract iron all the time. It works only when it is electrified.

● Things you'll need

Nail
Paper
Pliers
Tape
Battery
Paper clips
Insulated wire

■ Building an electromagnet

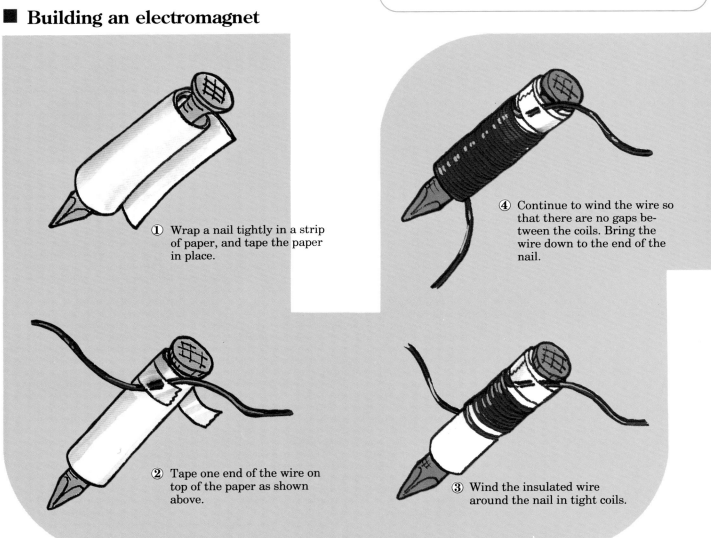

① Wrap a nail tightly in a strip of paper, and tape the paper in place.

② Tape one end of the wire on top of the paper as shown above.

③ Wind the insulated wire around the nail in tight coils.

④ Continue to wind the wire so that there are no gaps between the coils. Bring the wire down to the end of the nail.

36

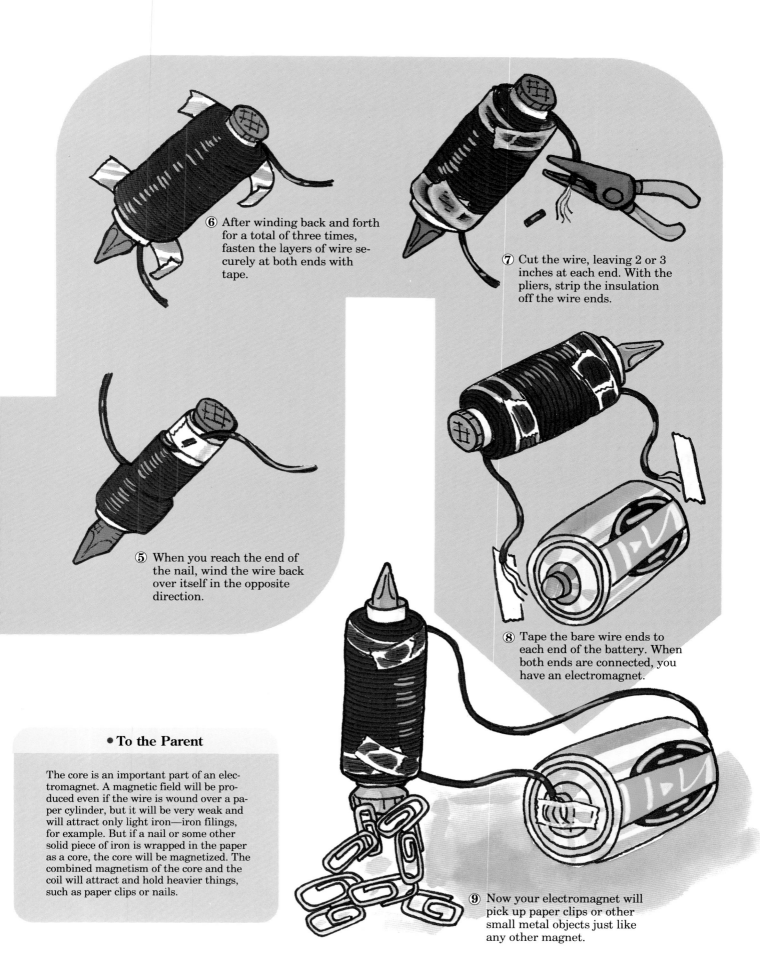

⑥ After winding back and forth for a total of three times, fasten the layers of wire securely at both ends with tape.

⑦ Cut the wire, leaving 2 or 3 inches at each end. With the pliers, strip the insulation off the wire ends.

⑤ When you reach the end of the nail, wind the wire back over itself in the opposite direction.

⑧ Tape the bare wire ends to each end of the battery. When both ends are connected, you have an electromagnet.

⑨ Now your electromagnet will pick up paper clips or other small metal objects just like any other magnet.

● **To the Parent**

The core is an important part of an electromagnet. A magnetic field will be produced even if the wire is wound over a paper cylinder, but it will be very weak and will attract only light iron—iron filings, for example. But if a nail or some other solid piece of iron is wrapped in the paper as a core, the core will be magnetized. The combined magnetism of the core and the coil will attract and hold heavier things, such as paper clips or nails.

Did You Know You Can Use Fruit to Make Electricity?

(ANSWER) Fruit by itself does not make electricity. But strips of zinc and copper, inserted into an acid fruit, will start a flow of electricity. If you wire the metal strips as shown here and connect them to a flashlight bulb, you will see how this works.

■ How electricity works

1. Connect the wire ends of the socket to one copper and one zinc strip. Stick the metal strips into an apple.
2. The zinc loses electrons *(blue)* to the apple acid *(green)*.
3. Hydrogen ions *(yellow)* from the acid try to remove electrons from both strips.

4. Copper loses electrons but replaces them right away by pulling in new ones from the zinc.
5. Electricity flows along the wires as electrons are pulled from the zinc strip to the copper strip, lighting the bulb.

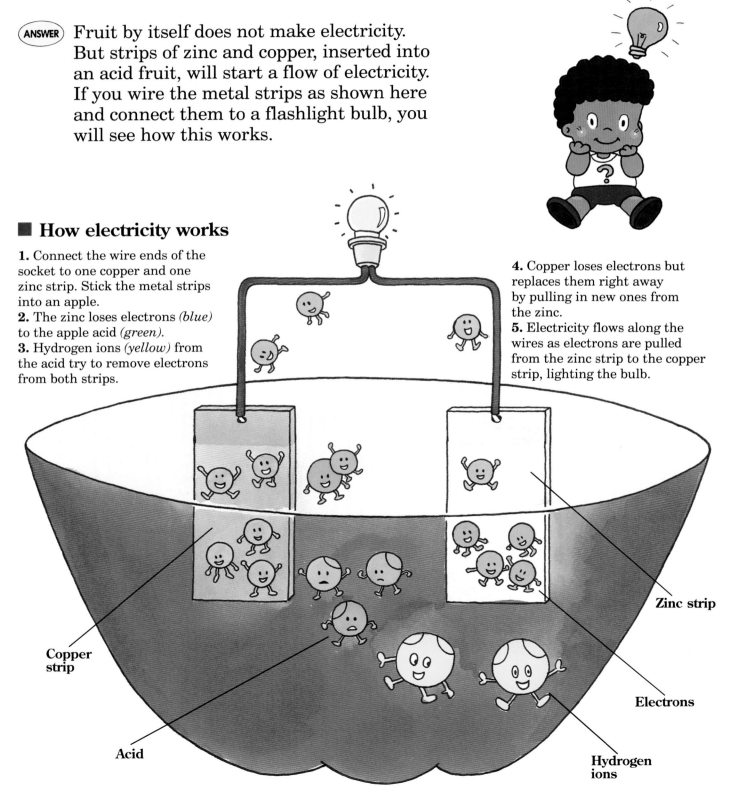

Zinc strip

Copper strip

Electrons

Acid

Hydrogen ions

■ Making a battery

A battery made from one apple is weak. You will get a stronger current if you use more than one apple. The apples can be connected to one another as shown below. The smaller the flashlight bulb is, the better the experiment works.

● Things you'll need

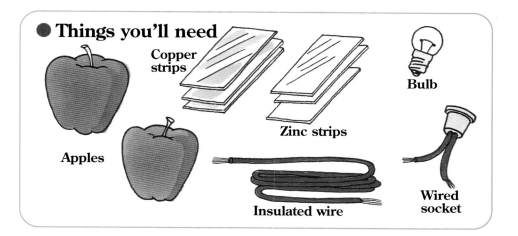

Copper strips

Zinc strips

Bulb

Apples

Insulated wire

Wired socket

▼ A battery made from apples

■ Try other fruit

You can also use lemons and grapefruits to make electricity. Even vegetables such as potatoes will work. The acid does not have to be strong in these fruits.

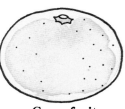

Grapefruit

Potato

Lemon

How Can a Plastic Rod Work like a Magnet?

(ANSWER) Electricity is a form of energy contained in many things, from lightning bolts to eels, from electric circuits to the human nervous system. You can see some of its effects in static electricity. When you rub plastic or rubber with wool, you create an electric charge that attracts or repels other objects.

● **Things you'll need**

Bits of paper

Plastic rod   Balloons   Wool cloth

■ A plastic attractor

Pass the plastic rod over small pieces of paper. If you don't have a plastic rod, use a plastic comb. The rod has not been charged. There is no attraction, and nothing happens.

Briskly rub the plastic rod with wool. Now the plastic is charged.

Pass the plastic rod over the paper again. This time the paper sticks to the rod. The charged plastic attracts the paper just as a magnet attracts iron or steel.

■ Why the paper sticks

▼Most materials have an equal number of positive and negative charges and are electrically neutral. Such material does not attract or repel other things.

▼When you rub plastic with wool, the negative charges from the wool move to the plastic.

◀When the plastic with its extra negative charges is brought close to the paper, it attracts the positive charges in the paper, causing the paper to stick to the plastic.

■ Charged balloons

Blow up two balloons and tie them with string. Rub them with wool. Hang one from the ceiling and bring the other one close. The dangling one will move away.

● To the Parent

The attraction between paper and plastic is caused by static electricity. When you rub the plastic with wool, the wool transfers negative charges to the plastic, which now has more negative than positive charges. The added negative charges attract the paper's positive charges and repel its negative charges. The attraction between the negatively charged plastic and the paper's positively charged surface makes the slips of paper jump to the plastic rod. Rubbing the balloons against the wool produces a negative charge on both balloons, causing them to repel rather than attract each other.

How Can You Make a Camera at Home?

ANSWER The simplest kind of camera is a box with a pinhole. Light entering through the pinhole makes images appear on the back wall of the box. You can make your own camera by using a box or by following the instructions below.

● Things you'll need

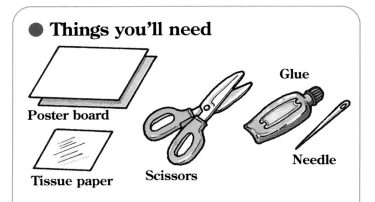

Poster board

Tissue paper

Scissors

Glue

Needle

■ A pinhole camera

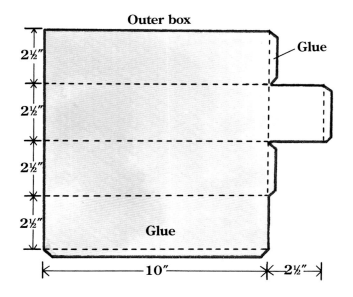

Outer box

Glue

2½"

2½"

2½"

2½"

Glue

|← —————10″———— →|←2½″→|

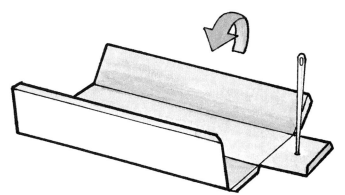

Draw the box on poster board as shown at left, and cut it out. With the help of a parent, punch a hole in the center of the flap. Bend the panels along the dotted lines, and glue the tabs in place. This is the outer box.

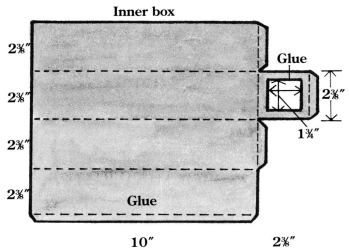

Inner box

2⅜"

2⅜"

2⅜"

2⅜"

Glue

Glue

2⅜"

1¾"

10″   2⅜″

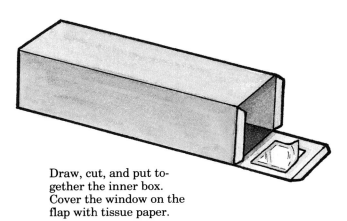

Draw, cut, and put together the inner box. Cover the window on the flap with tissue paper.

■ The camera and the human eye

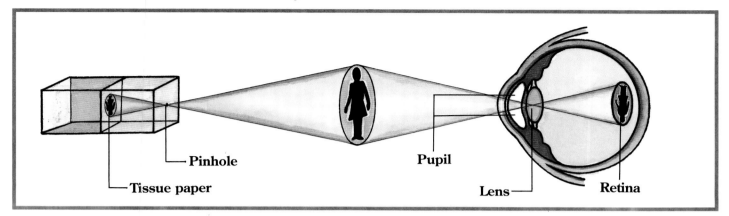

Pinhole

Tissue paper

Pupil

Lens

Retina

A camera and the human eye work in similar ways. The camera's pinhole acts like the lens of the eye. The tissue paper does the job of the retina, which is on the back wall of the eye. As light from an object passes through the lens, the light rays form an upside-down image on the retina.

▲ Fit the two boxes, as above, and you have a camera. Point the pinhole end at a scene, and see the image upside down on the tissue-paper window.

● To the Parent

This pinhole camera cannot take photographs, because tissue paper is taking the place of film. A pinhole camera with film would take somewhat blurry pictures, similar to the earliest photographs. By sliding the inner box in or out, as in a camera with a zoom lens, you can move the image closer or farther away. The image is projected upside down because light passing through the pinhole is bent, just as light entering the eye is bent by the lens, casting the image upside down on the retina.

What Is a Periscope?

ANSWER A periscope is an instrument for seeing around objects. Periscopes in submarines peer out of the water while the ship is under the waves. You can use a periscope to look over a fence or around a corner.

● **Things you'll need**

Poster board

Scissors

Mirrors

Glue

■ Building a periscope

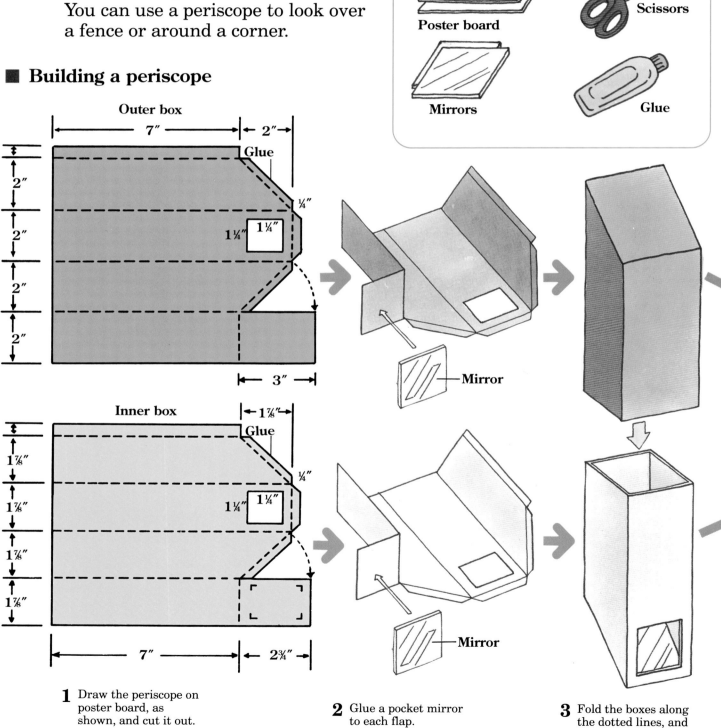

Outer box

7"

2"

Glue

2"

¼"

2"

1¼" 1¼"

2"

2"

3"

Inner box

1⅞"

Glue

1⅞"

¼"

1⅞"

1¼" 1¼"

1⅞"

1⅞"

7"

2¾"

Mirror

Mirror

1 Draw the periscope on poster board, as shown, and cut it out.

2 Glue a pocket mirror to each flap.

3 Fold the boxes along the dotted lines, and glue the tabs down.

44

■ Try different angles

By shifting the way the boxes are lined up, you can change your view.

▲ **Look straight ahead.**　▲ **Look to the side.**　▲ **Look behind you.**

4 When you fit the boxes into each other, your periscope is ready. Now you can look over, under, or around things. Don't aim the periscope at the sun, though. The mirrors reflect the sun so brightly you could damage your eyes.

●To the Parent

A periscope can see around obstacles because the image in the upper mirror is reflected into the lower mirror. When the light hits the mirror at a 45° angle, it bounces off the mirror at the same angle, making a 90° turn. If you cannot find pocket mirrors of the right size, use aluminum foil or Mylar instead.

Can You Do Tricks with Mirrors?

ANSWER A single mirror reflects the image of the object in front of it. But what happens when you add another mirror? Experiment with an object, such as the clock shown here, and two mirrors, and see how many reflections you can get.

● **Things you'll need**

Mirrors   Clock

■ A world of mirrors

By placing the mirrors at a right angle, you will see the clock reflected from three sides at the same time. Can you get more reflections?

In the illustration below, left, the mirrors reflect the clock five ways. How should you place the mirrors to get more reflections?

The illustration below, right, shows an endless series of clocks. What can you do to get the same effect?

①

②

③

A kaleidoscope

The colorful pattern inside a kaleidoscope is produced with mirrors. When you turn the kaleidoscope, the colored pieces inside shift to combine in new ways. Each new pattern is multiplied by reflections.

● **Things you'll need**

Mirrors   Tape   Scissors

Colored paper bits   Tissue paper

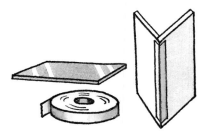

Tape three mirrors of the same size together to form a triangle.

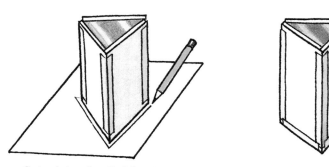

Cut a triangle of white tissue paper that is slightly larger than the mirror triangle, and tape the paper over one open end of the mirrors. Cut colored construction paper into small pieces.

Drop the colored bits of paper through the mirrors onto the tissue paper.

Look through the open end of your kaleidoscope, turning it gently, and watch the changing pattern.

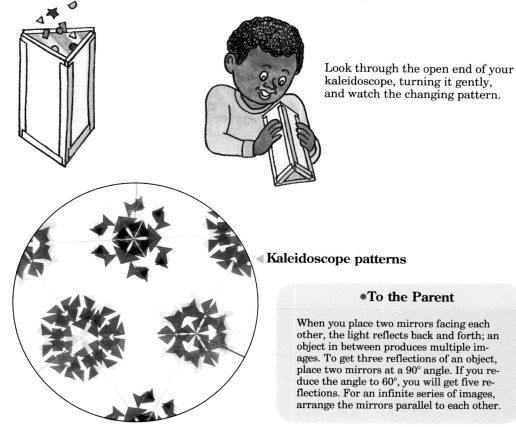

◄ **Kaleidoscope patterns**

●**To the Parent**

When you place two mirrors facing each other, the light reflects back and forth; an object in between produces multiple images. To get three reflections of an object, place two mirrors at a 90° angle. If you reduce the angle to 60°, you will get five reflections. For an infinite series of images, arrange the mirrors parallel to each other.

? Why Are Things Underwater Not Where You Think They Are?

ANSWER Light normally travels in a straight line. But sometimes it is bent or split by things that get in its way. Light passing through two clear materials—like air and water—bends where it leaves one material and enters the other. If an object is underwater, the light that is coming from the object bends at the surface of the water.

● **Things you'll need**

Bowls

Water

Coins   Scissors

Plastic wrap

Poster board

Corn syrup

■ Comparing coins

Place one coin in the first bowl and another coin in the second bowl in the same position. Fill one of the bowls with water and compare. Do the coins still seem to be in the same place?

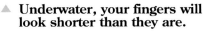

▲ Underwater, your fingers will look shorter than they are.

■ What happened?

When you look at the coin in the waterless bowl, light from the coin travels in a straight line to your eyes. But when the coin is covered by water, the light's path is bent at the border between the water and the air. The coin seems to be in a different position.

▲ **You cannot see the coin.**

▲ **Now you can see it.**

How Can Water Magnify?

The hardest part of making a water magnifying glass is holding the water in place. You can pour the water on plastic in a cardboard holder. If the water spills, try corn syrup instead. It will not flow away as easily as the water does.

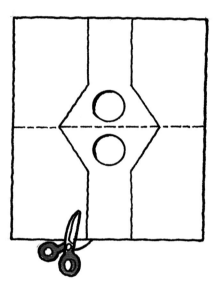

Draw the shape shown at right on poster board, and cut it out. Cut two circles for the lens, and fold the holder along the dotted line. Firmly tape a piece of plastic wrap over the inside of one hole, and bend the holder shut. Dribble drops of water onto the plastic to fill the hole.

Water

Plastic wrap

Look at the letters on a printed page with the water magnifying glass. Do the letters look bigger?

❓ How Does a Scale Work?

ANSWER A scale tells you how much an object weighs. Most scales have a spring that becomes longer or shorter depending on the weight pulling on it. You can make a simple scale from a box and a rubber band that acts like a spring.

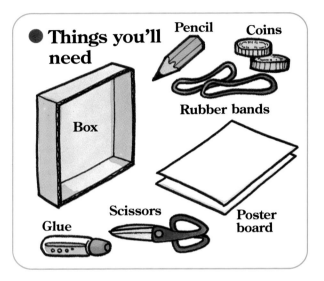

● **Things you'll need**

Pencil Coins

Box

Rubber bands

Glue Scissors Poster board

■ Making a scale

Cut two flaps in the center of the box's top and bottom. Bend the flaps out as shown below.

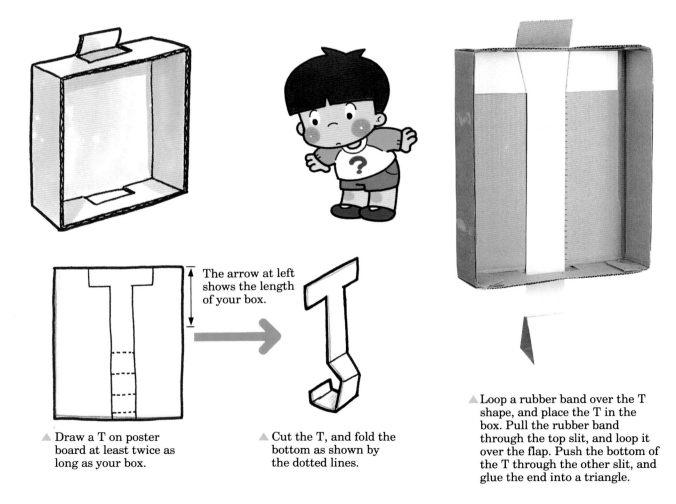

The arrow at left shows the length of your box.

▲ Draw a T on poster board at least twice as long as your box.

▲ Cut the T, and fold the bottom as shown by the dotted lines.

▲ Loop a rubber band over the T shape, and place the T in the box. Pull the rubber band through the top slit, and loop it over the flap. Push the bottom of the T through the other slit, and glue the end into a triangle.

■ Marking a scale

▽ Weigh a coin, and make a line under the T, as shown.

▽ Add a second coin of the same kind, and mark the box.

▽ Keep adding coins of the same kind, one at a time.

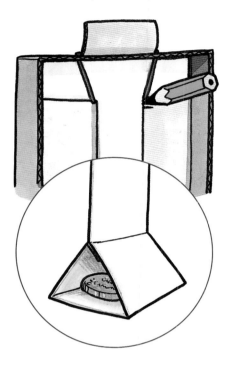

Mark the box after adding each coin for as long as the rubber band will stretch.

■ Weighing some things

Now you can weigh different objects. See how many paper clips are equal to one coin, or try heavier things, such as a pen or an eraser. Always hold your scale by the top flap so that the scale hangs straight.

▲ To weigh larger objects, add another box at the bottom, and make new marks.

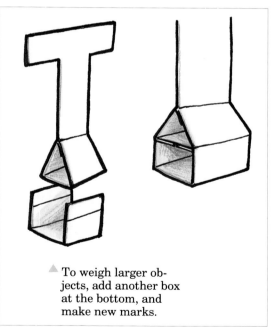

● To the Parent

This scale depends on the stretching and contracting of a rubber band. An ordinary scale would use a spring. A rubber band or a spring will always stretch the same distance if it is subjected to the same amount of force. When you know how much a spring will stretch from a known weight, you can weigh other objects.

What Is the Secret of Making Giant Soap Bubbles?

ANSWER Blowing beautiful, rainbow-colored soap bubbles is simple. All it takes is a mixture of soap and water and a loop to blow through. You can form larger bubbles by adding a sticky substance that will help the bubbles hold their shape. Experiment with different amounts of ingredients to find the mixture you like best.

● **Things you'll need**

Glass   Straw   Soap   Paper cup

Scissors   Yarn   Wire

Poster board   Sugar   Oil   Glycerin

■ How to go about it

Dissolve soap powder or flakes in water. Add a teaspoon of sugar and stir. Cut straws in different shapes as shown at right. Dip a straw into the liquid, and gently blow from the uncut end. Your bubbles will be larger than any you made before. Which straw gives you the largest bubble?

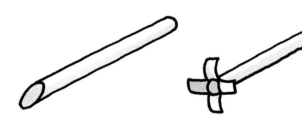

▲ Cut the end of the straw at an angle.

▲ Split the straw's end into four sections, and fold them out.

Soap   Sugar

■ Try other shapes

When you make openings of different shapes and sizes for your straw, the soap bubbles will also take on different shapes.

Glycerin

◄ Add a few drops of glycerin to the soap-and-water mixture. Glycerin is thick and sticky and will hold the bubbles together.

Oil

▲ Cooking oil feels similar to glycerin. If you add a few drops of oil instead of glycerin, though, the bubbles will not hold together. The oil causes the water to lose its tension.

■ New shapes

▲ Experiment with different shapes of bubble makers. Roll poster board into a cone or punch a hole in the bottom of a paper cup. These shapes will make giant soap bubbles. What others can you make?

▲ Wrap a wire loop tightly with yarn. Dip the loop into the bubble solution, then draw the loop through the air as shown below. By moving gently you will get a huge soap bubble.

● To the Parent

The size and strength of soap bubbles depend on the concentration of the mixture. Add a little soap at a time to a glass of water, testing the solution by blowing through a straw until the concentration suits you. Both glycerin and sugar increase the viscosity of the solution and make bubbles harder to break, but oil causes the bubble mixture to lose its surface tension so that bubbles cannot form.

❓ Why Does Ice Melt Faster When Salt Is Sprinkled on It?

ANSWER When you sprinkle salt on ice, the ice will melt faster than normal. This is because salt lowers the melting point of ice. That means that ice can melt at temperatures below 32° F. Normally water freezes at 32° F.

● **Things you'll need**

Ice

Salt

Glasses

Outdoor thermometer

■ Different temperatures

Compare the melting of ice alone with the melting of ice with salt. Check the temperatures of the meltwater with an outdoor thermometer. The salt-and-ice mixture melts faster, but the temperature of its meltwater is lower than that of the ice water without salt.

Ice mixed with salt

▲ Place ice cubes in a glass, and add about one part of salt to three parts of ice.

▲ As the ice melts, the thermometer shows temperatures below 32° F.

▲ When the ice is nearly melted, the thermometer reads as low as 0° F.

Ice

▲ Fill a glass with ice cubes, but do not add salt.

▲ After a little while, the ice begins to melt. The thermometer reads 32° F.

▲ When the ice is almost all gone, the thermometer still reads 32° F.

■ What is going on?

When you sprinkle salt on ice, the salt helps water molecules begin to break free from the ice crystals and the ice starts to melt.

■ Falling temperatures

Energy is needed to break the forces that hold water molecules together as ice. This energy is taken from the surrounding water in the form of heat. This causes the water to become colder as the ice melts.

● **To the Parent**

When you add salt to ice, the salt's sodium and chloride separate and sodium and chloride ions attach to water molecules. These ions break the intermolecular forces that hold ice crystals together. As a result, water molecules break away from the ice crystals and cause the ice to melt. The energy needed to break the intermolecular forces is called heat of fusion and comes from the surrounding water. This process lowers the water temperature.

❓ Why Do Ponds Freeze at the Top?

(ANSWER) Although all liquids start to freeze from the top, only water ice stays on top. All other kinds of ice sink to the bottom. When water is cooled to below 39° F., it strays from the normal pattern in which solid things are heavier than liquid ones. When cooled below 39° F., water grows lighter and less dense. It rises to the top, where it is exposed to colder air, which freezes it. This ice, which is less dense than water, floats.

● **Things you'll need**

Outdoor thermometer

Sugar

Glass

■ Water temperatures

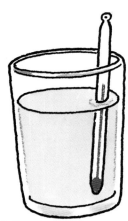  

▲ Fill a glass with water, and place a thermometer in the water. Put the glass in the freezer.

▲ Within a few minutes the temperature will drop to 39° F.

▲ If you leave the glass in the freezer, ice will begin to form on top. But the water at the bottom is still 39° F.

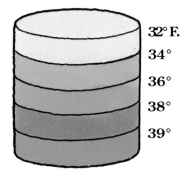

32° F.

34°

36°

38°

39°

The density of water changes with its temperature. As water begins to freeze, the temperature at the top is different from that at the bottom. The experiment above shows that the water at the bottom of the glass stays at 39° F. Water is heaviest at that temperature. Colder water begins to rise to the top.

What Happens If You Freeze Sugar Water?

Water still freezes from the top even when sugar is dissolved in it. But if you taste the ice as soon as it has formed, you will find that it is not sweet. What happens to the sugar?

▲ Dissolve a teaspoonful of sugar in a glass of water.

▶ Put the glass with the sugar water in the freezer. As soon as ice begins to form on top, take it out and taste it.

■ Why the ice isn't sweet

Ice

Water   Sugar

Sugar water contains molecules of water and of sugar. The bonds holding together water molecules are stronger than those of sugar molecules. The sugar molecules are crowded out when sugar water freezes.

● To the Parent

At temperatures above 39° F., water becomes more dense as it cools, reaching its greatest density at 39° F. As the temperature goes below 39° F., water expands, becoming less dense as it cools. This water will rise to the top, becoming even less dense as it freezes into a layer of solid ice.

? Why Does the Pressure Increase the Deeper You Go in Water?

ANSWER When you dive into deep water you can feel the pressure of the water against your body. The farther down you go beneath the surface, the harder the water presses against you. The pressure comes from the weight of the water above you.

● **Things you'll need**

Awl

Plastic bag

Tape

Plastic bottle

Water tank

■ Checking pressures

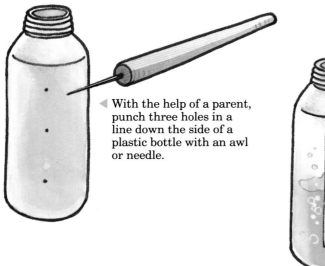

◀ With the help of a parent, punch three holes in a line down the side of a plastic bottle with an awl or needle.

▲ Tape the holes shut, and fill the bottle with water.

▲ Pull off the tape. The water from the bottom hole shoots out the farthest because the pressure is greatest there.

■ Making strong dams

Water pressure plays an important role in building dams. Dams are built to hold back rivers and must be strongest at the bottom where the pressure is greatest.

▲ Arrows show increasing pressure

▲ Water pressure is highest at the bottom

■ Fish feel pressure too

In the depths of the ocean, the water's pressure is enormously strong. Even so, a few creatures manage to live at the very bottom. The pressure there is so high that if these creatures are brought to the surface, they will burst apart, because the pressure they are used to no longer exists.

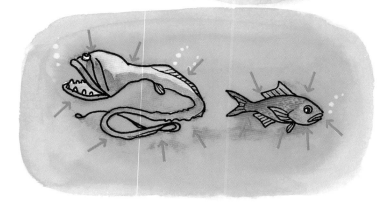

MINI-DATA

Slip a plastic bag over your hand, and put it in a water tank. The bag will cling tightly, showing how pressure works.

●To the Parent

Water pressure increases with depth at a rate of 35 pounds per cubic inch. The bottom of the ocean, tens of thousands of feet deep in some places, is subjected to tremendous water pressure, as much as 8 tons per cubic inch at times. Submersible vehicles for research on the ocean floor must be specially designed so they will not be crushed by that overwhelming force.

How Can You Make an Egg Float?

ANSWER Most solid objects will sink if you drop them in water. Fresh eggs will sink to the bottom of a glass of water. But if you drop an egg in a glass of salt water, the egg will float. See for yourself when you try the experiment described below.

● **Things you'll need**

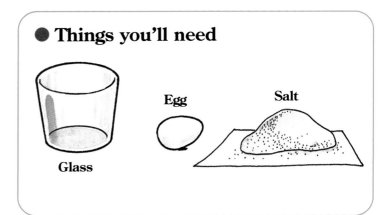

Glass   Egg   Salt

■ Adding salt

1 Drop a fresh egg into a glass of water. The egg will sink.

2 Start adding salt to the water.

3 Stir the water gently to dissolve the salt, and keep adding salt.

4 When the water gets really salty, the egg floats up.

■ Why does it float?

The egg floats in salt water because the egg is less dense and less heavy than salt water. Compare the weight of the egg with the weight of the water it displaces in the illustrations below.

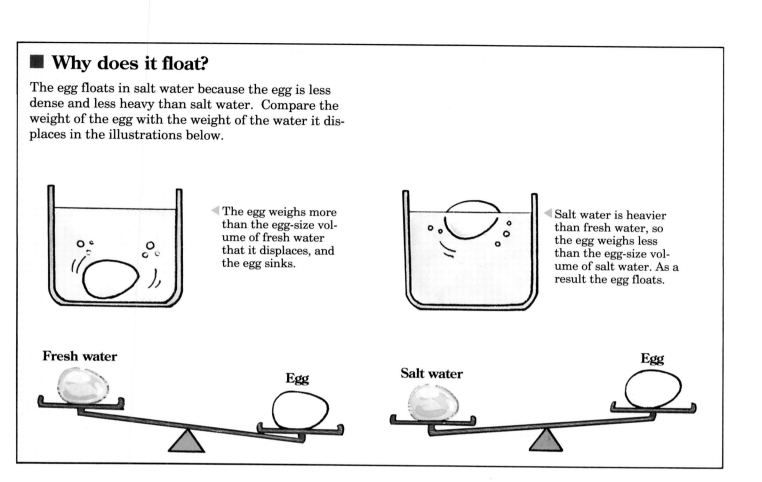

◀ The egg weighs more than the egg-size volume of fresh water that it displaces, and the egg sinks.

◀ Salt water is heavier than fresh water, so the egg weighs less than the egg-size volume of salt water. As a result the egg floats.

Fresh water

Egg

Salt water

Egg

● To the Parent

An object immersed in water is buoyed upward by a force that is equal to the weight of water the object displaces. The larger the object, the more upward force there is. The amount of buoyant force is independent of the weight of the object. However, when the buoyant force is equal to the weight of the object, the object will float. In this experiment, the volume and the mass of the egg are constant, but the masses of the egg-size volumes of fresh water and salt water differ. Buoyant force is dependent on the volume of the object and the density of the liquid.

Did You Know You Can Grow Your Own Salt Crystals?

ANSWER If you look at grains of salt under a magnifying glass, you will discover that they are shaped like cubes. Each cube is a crystal. In the experiment below you can make tiny salt crystals grow larger.

● Things you'll need

Salt

Glass

Stirrer

Thread

Plate

■ Growing crystals

1 Begin by adding a teaspoonful of salt to a glass of water. Stir until the salt dissolves. Keep adding salt until no more will dissolve.

2 Pour a little of the salt water onto a plate, and save the remainder. Set the plate in the sun or some other warm, dry place to let the water evaporate.

■ How crystals form

As the water evaporates, the salt remains and takes its crystal shape again.

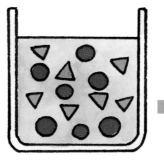

▲ Dissolved salt is evenly distributed in a glass of water.

▲ When most of the water has evaporated, the salt recrystallizes.

3 When all the water has evaporated, only the dry salt crystals are left.

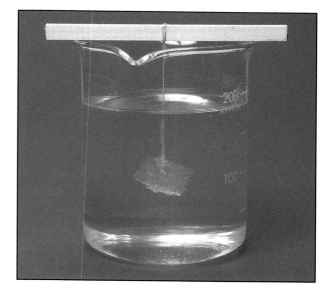

4 Pick out the largest crystal, and tie a thread around it. Tie the other end of the thread to a stick or a pencil, and lay the stick across the glass of salt water. Let the crystal hang into the water. Leave the glass in a warm place for about a week. The crystal will grow larger.

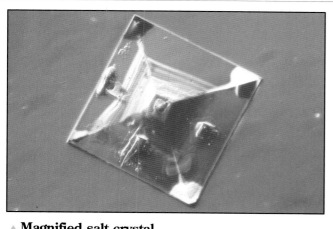

▲ **Magnified salt crystal**

●**To the Parent**

A crystal of salt consists of one sodium ion surrounded by four chlorine ions. Each chlorine ion, in turn, is surrounded by four sodium ions. Seed crystals for the experimental growth of larger crystals are made by dissolving salt in water, which is left to evaporate. During evaporation the sodium and chlorine ions, which were separated by water molecules, recombine and form larger crystals. If these crystals are then suspended in dense, supersaturated salt water, they will form even larger crystals as the water evaporates. Crystals that are grown this way are free of impurities.

How Can You Power a Toy Car with Rubber Bands?

ANSWER You can build a car from nothing more than a milk carton and rubber bands. The car is powered by the springiness of a stretched rubber band and will run very fast for a short distance. If your friends build their own cars, you can race with them.

Things you'll need

Milk carton

Rubber bands

Scissors

Tape

Sticks

■ Rubber band engine

1 Cut the milk carton in half, as shown by the dotted line in the illustration.

2 Cut a notch at the bottom front to hold a rubber band.

3 Push the sticks, or two pencils, through the milk carton, about ½ inch from the bottom, to make the axles.

4 Loop a rubber band around the rear axle and tape it. Twist it to take up the slack, and hook the loose end into the notch at the front.

5 Cut the other half of the carton lengthwise into four equal strips. Tape the end of one to the end of an axle, and wind to form a wheel. Stretch a rubber band around it. Make the other three. To make the car go, turn the rear axle to loop the band around it, and let the car loose.

■ Making a boat

With just one axle and two paddles instead of wheels, you can make the car into a paddleboat.

Make two flat paddles from milk carton strips and fasten them with rubber bands as shown. Arrange them on the axle—one upright, one flat—so that they will take turns hitting the water.

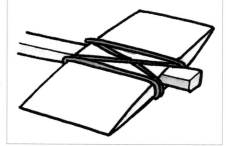

● **To the Parent**

Toys made from milk cartons are waterproof, but they often are too light. If the car's wheels spin or the bow of the boat lifts out of the water, try placing weights at those points. The axles may not turn easily until the holes in the carton are worn down. These toys are powered by the elasticity of the stretched and twisted rubber bands. You may want to show your child how rubber bands, like all elastic materials, go back to their original shape after they have been stretched.

What New Things Can You Make with Modeling Clay?

ANSWER Modeling clay is a good material for making toys because you can form it into any shape you like. You can also use it as a weight to make things move in funny ways.

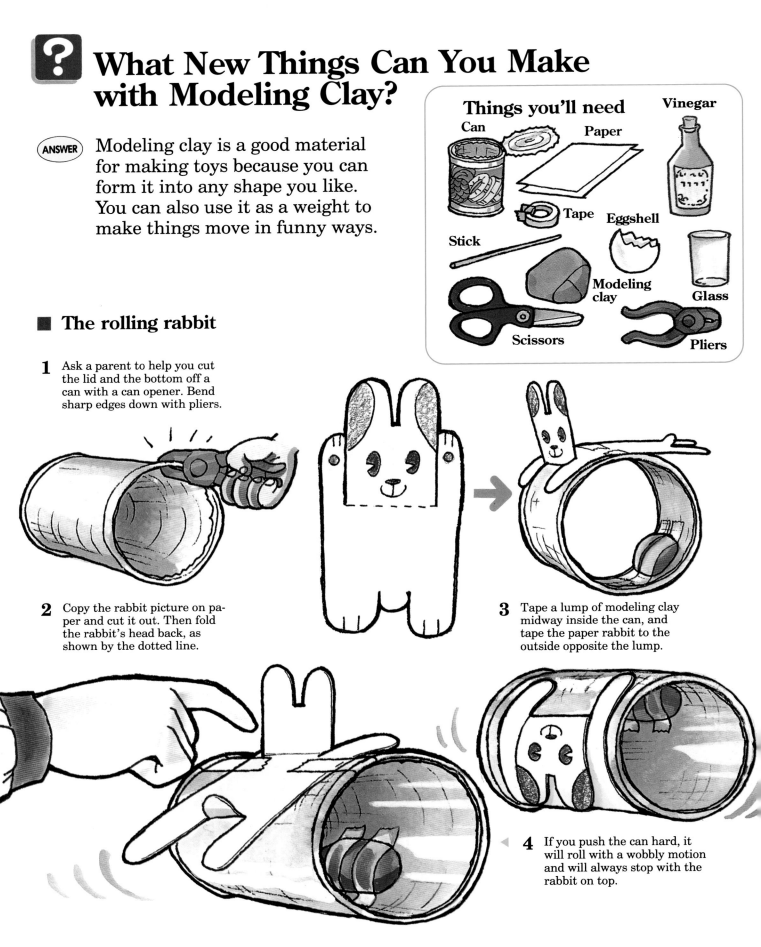

Things you'll need

Can
Paper
Vinegar
Tape
Eggshell
Stick
Modeling clay
Glass
Scissors
Pliers

■ The rolling rabbit

1 Ask a parent to help you cut the lid and the bottom off a can with a can opener. Bend sharp edges down with pliers.

2 Copy the rabbit picture on paper and cut it out. Then fold the rabbit's head back, as shown by the dotted line.

3 Tape a lump of modeling clay midway inside the can, and tape the paper rabbit to the outside opposite the lump.

4 If you push the can hard, it will roll with a wobbly motion and will always stop with the rabbit on top.

66

■ A swaying cat

The next time someone in your family is cooking with eggs, save the rounded bottom half of a shell. Soak the eggshell in vinegar.

When the eggshell has soaked for about two hours, it will have softened enough so that you can cut it with scissors. Cut the ragged edges so the rim looks smooth and even.

1 Fill the eggshell with modeling clay, taking care not to break the shell.

2 Place a wooden stick, a skewer, or a pencil upright in the center of the modeling clay.

3 Draw a cat face on construction paper and then cut it out.

4 Tape the cat face to the stick.

5 Push the cat toy with your fingers. It will sway back and forth but will not tip over.

● To the Parent

These experiments demonstrate principles about the center of gravity. The distribution of the mass of an object determines the position of its center of gravity. The rolling can will always stop with the rabbit on top because almost all the toy's mass is contained in the heavy lump of clay. Similarly, the cat toy is stable because the center of mass is lower than the physical center of the toy.

 What Is a Lever?

(ANSWER) A seesaw lifts heavy adults as easily as small children because the center of the board swivels around a fixed point and the far end carries the weight. The seesaw is, in fact, a simple machine, called a lever. Bottle openers, nail pullers, and crowbars are also levers.

■ The power of a lever

Lay a stick under the center of a long, narrow board. You have now made a lever. Stack books at one end of the board, and press down on the other end. You will now be able to lift the books with this lever, but you will have to push with some effort.

● **Things you'll need**

Board

Stick

Books

◀ Put the stick under one end of the board and the books on the other end. You cannot lift the books, even if you push down on the end with all your might.

▼ Slide the stick closer to the end where the books are, but not directly under them. Now you can lift the books with very little effort.

■ Try it on a seesaw

Compare lifting a stack of books with your arms and lifting the same stack on a seesaw. Which way is easier?

△ Place the books midway along one end of the seesaw, as shown above. Push down on the other end. The books lift easily. The closer they are to the center point, the easier it is to lift them.

One of the first people to recognize the power of the lever was the ancient Greek mathematician Archimedes. He was speaking of the lever when he said, "Give me a place to stand on, and I will move the earth."

■ Everyday levers

The lever action in a nail puller can pull out a nail with much less effort than a person pulling a nail straight up with pliers.

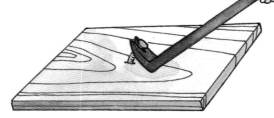

● **To the Parent**

A lever is a simple machine, consisting of a narrow beam that turns around a fixed point, called a fulcrum. By placing an object at one point on the beam and applying a force at another point, a person can lift an object with less effort than by picking it up. This is called a mechanical advantage. For the greatest mechanical advantage, the beam must be long and the load must be close to the fulcrum. Scissors, pliers, three-hole punches, and tweezers are also levers.

? Does a String Telephone Work?

(ANSWER) You can build a play telephone that sends your voice the same way a real phone does. Your voice travels over tight strings into the receiver. You can build the receivers as shown opposite, top right, or you can use paper or plastic-foam cups.

● **Things you'll need**

Scissors
Tape
Poster board
Toothpick
String
Tissue paper

■ A telephone network

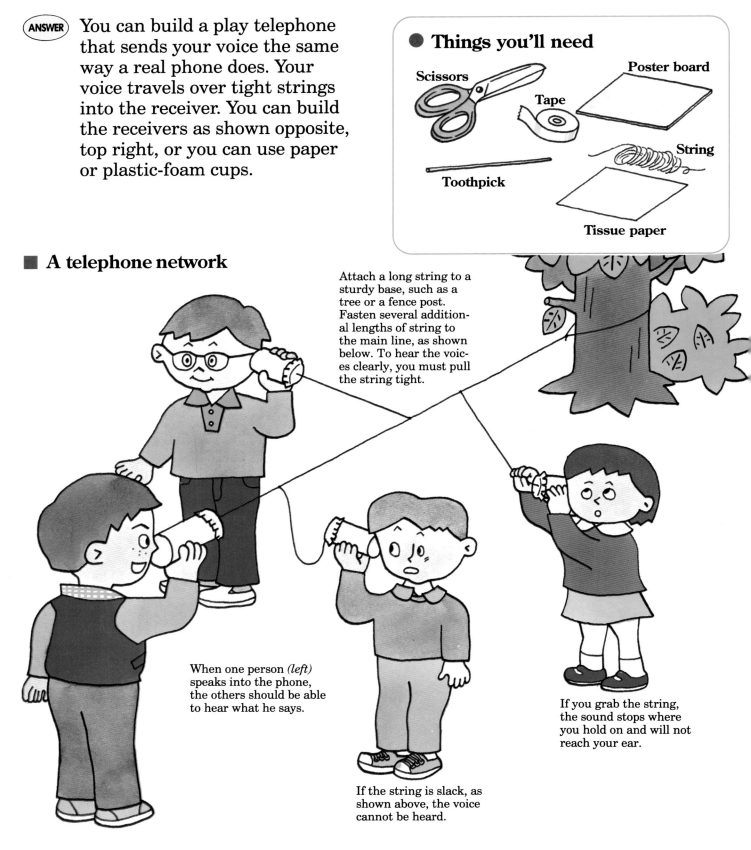

Attach a long string to a sturdy base, such as a tree or a fence post. Fasten several additional lengths of string to the main line, as shown below. To hear the voices clearly, you must pull the string tight.

When one person (*left*) speaks into the phone, the others should be able to hear what he says.

If the string is slack, as shown above, the voice cannot be heard.

If you grab the string, the sound stops where you hold on and will not reach your ear.

70

■ Making a telephone

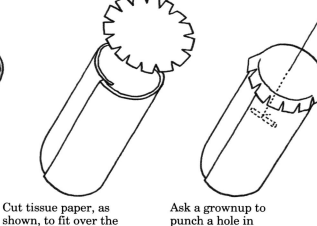

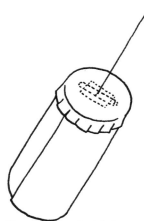

Cut a rectangle from poster board and tape the ends together to form a cylinder.

Cut tissue paper, as shown, to fit over the end of the cylinder. Do not tape it down yet.

Ask a grownup to punch a hole in the center. Thread the string through the hole and tie the end to half a toothpick.

Tape the toothpick in place on the paper. Then tape the tissue paper to the cylinder. Now you have a telephone receiver.

 How Can You Hear?

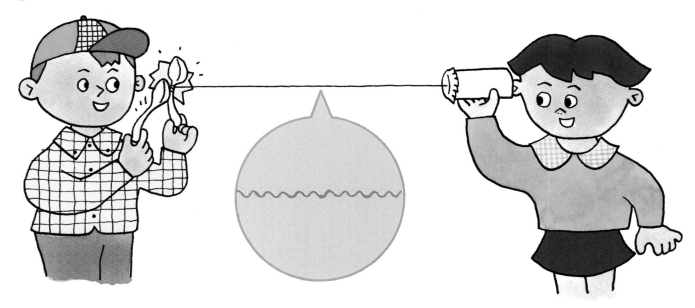

Tie a spoon to one end of a piece of string and tie a receiver to the other end. Hold the string tight, and then tap the spoon. The string will vibrate and transmit sound. In a real telephone, wires transmit voices in the same way.

● To the Parent

Sound sets up a succession of vibrations that make the air vibrate. These vibrations reach the ear and cause the eardrum to vibrate; that's when you hear a sound. The string telephone lets you see the process when the vibrations are transferred to a string. But if you grab the string or let it go slack, the string cannot carry the vibrations, and you will not hear any sound.

How Does Sound Travel through the Air?

ANSWER If you strike an object, it will vibrate. This, in turn, causes the air around it to vibrate. The vibrations travel through the air and reach your ear. The eardrum begins to vibrate, telling the brain that a certain kind of sound has been heard.

● **Things you'll need**

Glasses

Water

Thin wire

■ Good vibrations

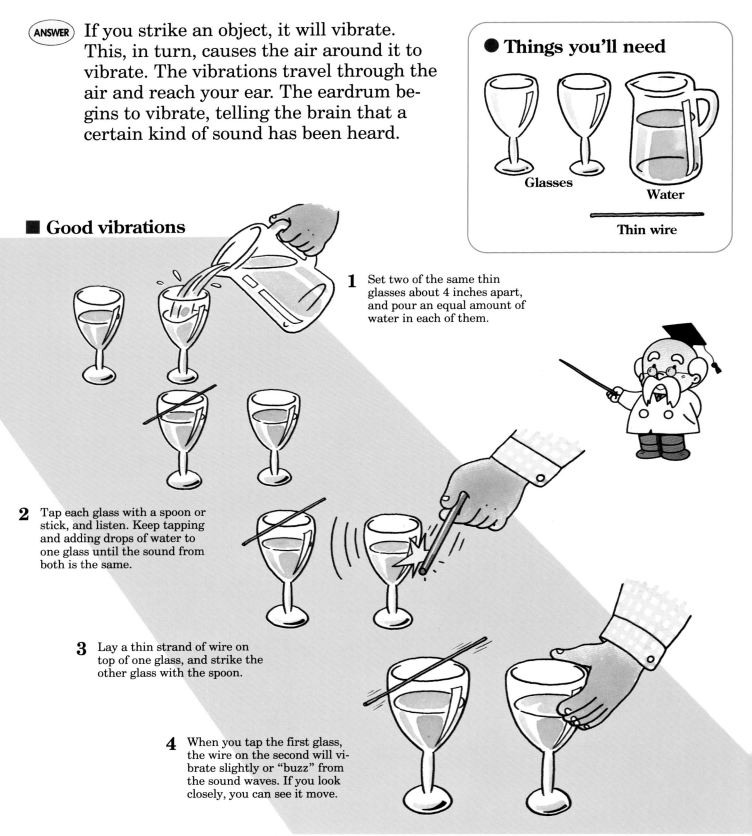

1 Set two of the same thin glasses about 4 inches apart, and pour an equal amount of water in each of them.

2 Tap each glass with a spoon or stick, and listen. Keep tapping and adding drops of water to one glass until the sound from both is the same.

3 Lay a thin strand of wire on top of one glass, and strike the other glass with the spoon.

4 When you tap the first glass, the wire on the second will vibrate slightly or "buzz" from the sound waves. If you look closely, you can see it move.

72

■ How sound carries in water

Clap two stones together and listen. Repeat it underwater. Can you tell a difference in the sound? The sound travels faster underwater than above water.

■ Speed of sound

The speed of sound changes depending on the things it travels through. Vibrations through air are fast, but sound travels faster through liquids. The speed increases when sound travels through solids.

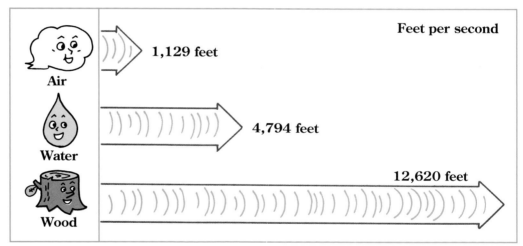

Feet per second

Air — 1,129 feet

Water — 4,794 feet

Wood — 12,620 feet

MINI-DATA

In outer space there is no air to carry the vibrations of sound. That means space is silent.

●**To the Parent**

Sound waves travel like ripples in a pond. When you tap the first glass, you set up ripples of vibrations in the second glass. Although the wire's motion is minute, you can see it. Sound travels faster through water and wood than through air because the molecules that transmit sound in water and wood are more densely packed than the loose molecules of air. The denser a material, the more easily vibrations pass from one molecule to the next. Sound does not travel in a vacuum; so outer space is silent.

Can You Join Two Balls by Blowing at Them?

ANSWER When you blow toward a light object, you usually blow it farther away. But by aiming the stream of air in just the right way, you can also bring things together by blowing. See if you can do the experiments that appear on these pages.

● **Things you'll need**

Ping-Pong balls

Straw

String

Tape

Paper clips

Balloon

Fan

■ **Powers of attraction**

Place two Ping-Pong balls on a table so that they are a short distance apart.

Blow air between the balls through a straw. The balls move toward each other, not apart.

Tape a piece of string around one ball, and hang it near a faucet. Turn the water on, and watch the ball move toward it.

◼ Balloon on the rise

If you blow up a balloon, it will not rise on its own. Do you know how to make it rise?

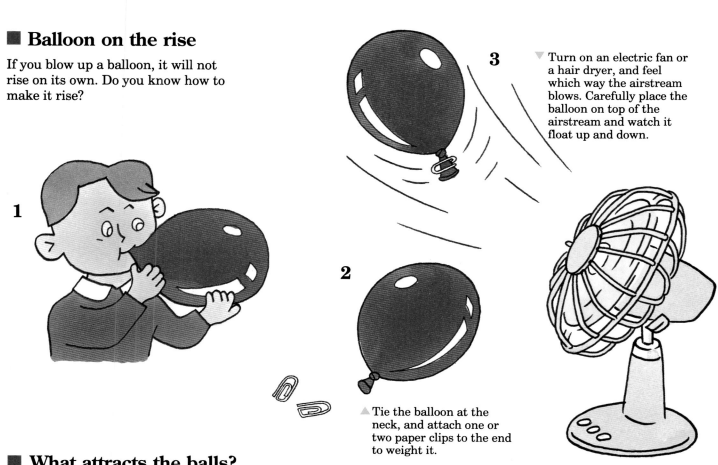

1

2
▲ Tie the balloon at the neck, and attach one or two paper clips to the end to weight it.

3 ▼ Turn on an electric fan or a hair dryer, and feel which way the airstream blows. Carefully place the balloon on top of the airstream and watch it float up and down.

◼ What attracts the balls?

Like all objects, the Ping-Pong balls are affected by air pressure. When you blow between the balls, the air between them is pushed away, allowing pressure from the sides to push the balls in, as shown below.

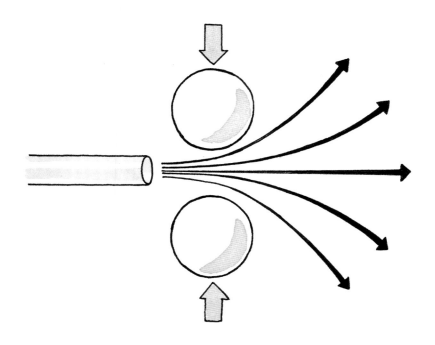

What Tricks Can You Play with Coins?

ANSWER If you would like to play new tricks on your friends, here are some ways to use coins. You may have to practice before you get these experiments to work. Your aim and the force you use must be just right to do the tricks.

■ A coin drop

Place an index card on top of a glass of water and put a coin on top of the card. Can you drop the coin into the glass without lifting the index card?

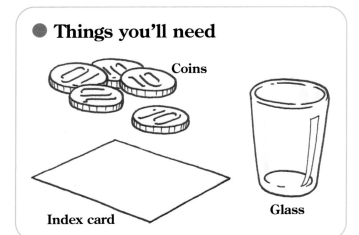

● Things you'll need

Coins

Index card

Glass

▲ Flick the edge of the index card sharply with your finger. The card will fly out from under the coin, and the coin, instead of moving with it, will drop into the water.

■ A chain reaction

Line up several coins in a straight row. From about a foot away, flick a single coin so that it will hit one end of the row.

▲ If you used the right amount of force, the new coin joined the line. But the coin at the far end was knocked away.

■ Using two coins

If you hit the same row of coins with two coins, two will fly off the back end, and the new coins will line up at the front.

● **To the Parent**

The coin experiments demonstrate Newton's laws of motion. The first law of motion states that an object at rest tends to remain at rest and an object in motion tends to remain in motion. The coin on the index card remains stationary, while the index card flies away. Gravity drops the coin into the glass. The row of coins demonstrates Newton's third law of motion, which describes changes in motion caused by the transfer of momentum in collisions. When the coin collides with the row of coins and stops, its momentum is transferred down the line of coins until it reaches the last coin, which then moves away from the others.

Can You Turn a Glass of Water Upside Down?

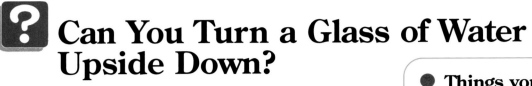

ANSWER You can turn a glass of water upside down without spilling a drop. All you need is an index card to cover the top. Find out how to do this trick by following the steps below.

● Things you'll need

Glass

Index card

Long, narrow board

Water

Newspaper

■ A wet experiment

Fill a glass with water, and place the index card on top.

Press down on the glass and card, between both hands.

■ The immovable paper

Place a long, thin board on a desk, and spread a newspaper on top of it.

With a quick chop, hit the board. No matter how hard you try, you can't lift the paper.

Holding the index card firmly in place, quickly turn the glass upside down.

Pull your bottom hand away. The water won't spill out.

■ No spills?

Air pressure alone is holding the water back. The air pressure is stronger than the weight of the water pushing against the index card, and the water does not spill.

? What Are These?

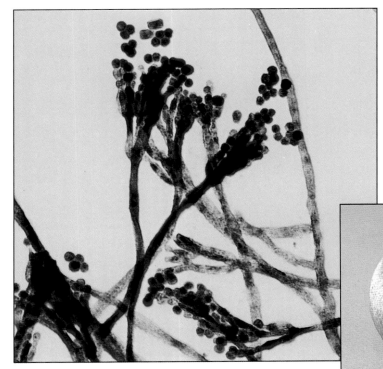

▲ Microscopic view of mold

■ Green mold

The same green mold you see on the rotten orange below looks like a green plant under the microscope at left. Molds are part of the plant kingdom but don't grow in soil; they live as parasites on other plants and animals and absorb nutrients from them.

▲ A moldy orange

▲ A rusty nail

▲ Enlarged view of rust

■ Rust on a nail

Rust is the reddish coating on iron exposed to moist air or water. Once rust has formed, it will slowly eat through the metal until the metal falls apart. Put a nail in a dish of water, and see how quickly rust appears.

● To the Parent

Mold is a fungus, a class of spore-producing plants that cannot make food through photosynthesis but live as parasites. Rust forms a brittle coating that flakes off to expose more iron to the oxidizing process.

Growing-Up Album

Which One Would You Use?

Which instrument should the children on the opposite page be using? Match each of the instruments numbered 1 through 6 with the pictures labeled A through F.

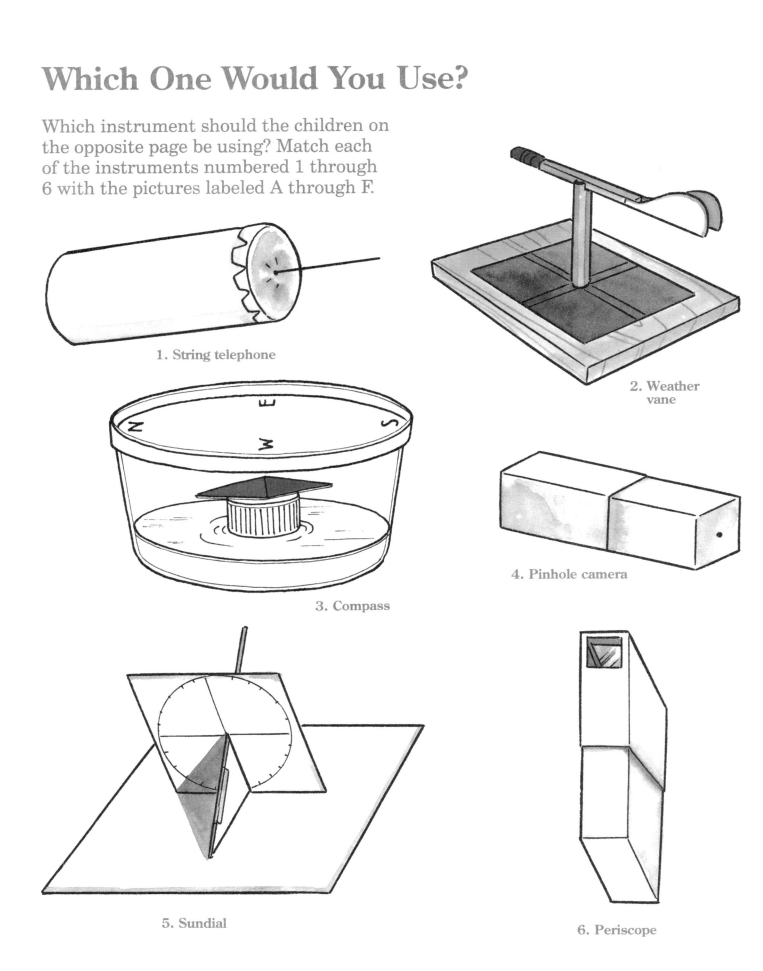

1. String telephone

2. Weather vane

3. Compass

4. Pinhole camera

5. Sundial

6. Periscope

A. Something that tells time

C. Something that shows wind direction

B. Something that shows an image

D. Something that sends voices

E. Something that lets you look over a fence

F. Something that tells you direction

Answers: (A)—(5); (B)—(4); (C)—(2); (D)—(1); (E)—(6); (F)—(3).

Where Do You Taste It?

You can taste the four basic flavors on different parts of your tongue. Where can you taste the flavor of each food marked A through D the strongest?

1. Tip of tongue

2. Back of tongue

3. Sides of tongue

4. Tip and front sides of tongue

A. Cake

B. Salt

C. Coffee

D. Pickles

Answers: (A)—(1); (B)—(4); (C)—(2); (D)—(3).

Which One Conducts Electricity?

Can you tell which objects shown on this page will cause the circuit tester to light up? Mark the objects that conduct electricity with an O in the box and those that do not with an X.

Can

Modeling clay

Water

Book

Salt water

Answers: Modeling clay—X; can—O; water—X; book—X; salt water—O.

Which One Shows the Right Image?

When you look into a mirror, you see yourself reflected exactly as you look. In the illustrations below, one mirror is wrong. Mark an O in the boxes under the mirrors that show the right image and an X in the box under the wrong reflection.

1

2

3

Answers: (1)—X; (2)—O; (3)—O.

86

What Makes the Biggest Bubbles?

There are three soap bubble mixtures in the illustrations below. Which mixture will make the largest soap bubbles? Mark an O in the boxes for a good mixture and an X for a bad one. You can also increase bubble size if you use straws of different shapes. Which of the straws marked 1 through 3 will make big bubbles? Mark the good ones with an O, the bad ones with an X.

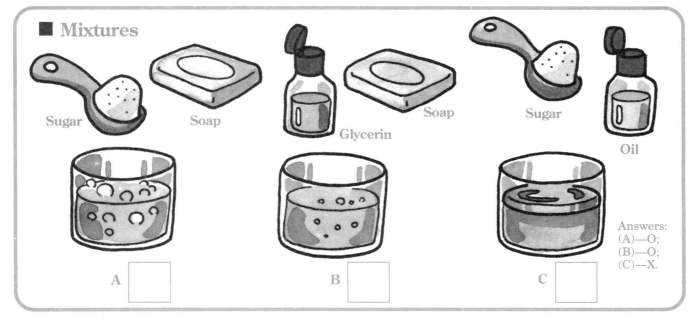

■ **Mixtures**

Sugar   Soap

Glycerin   Soap

Sugar   Oil

Answers:
(A)—O;
(B)—O;
(C)—X.

A ☐   B ☐   C ☐

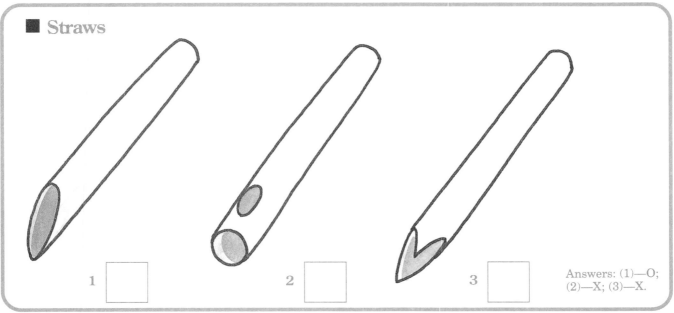

■ **Straws**

1 ☐   2 ☐   3 ☐

Answers: (1)—O;
(2)—X; (3)—X.

A Child's First Library of Learning

Staff for
SIMPLE EXPERIMENTS

Editorial Director: Karin Kinney
Editorial Coordinator: Marike van der Veen
Editorial Assistant: Mary M. Saxton
Production Manager: Marlene Zack
Copyeditors: Heidi A. Fritschel, Judy Klein
Picture Coordinator: David A. Herod
Production: Celia Beattie
Supervisor of Quality Control: James King
Assistant Supervisor of Quality Control: Miriam Newton
Library: Louise D. Forstall

Design/Illustration: Antonio Alcalá, John Jackson,
    David Neal Wiseman
Special Contributor (Art): Al Kettler
Photography: Cover: Roger Foley; 1 and 23 Roger Foley
Overread: Barbara Klein
Consultant: Andrew Pogan is a high-school teacher of chemistry
    and physics in Montgomery County, Maryland.

Library of Congress Cataloging-in-Publication Data
Simple Experiments.
    p.   cm. – (A Child's First Library of Learning)
    ISBN 0-8094-9470-1.
    1. Science—Experiments—Juvenile literature. [1. Science—
Experiments. 2. Experiments.] I. Series.
Q164.S56 1994
507'8—dc20   94-2319
                                                        CIP
                                                        AC

TIME-LIFE for CHILDREN ®

Managing Editor: Patricia Daniels
Editorial Directors: Jean Burke Crawford, Allan Fallow,
    Karin Kinney, Sara Mark
Senior Art Director: Sue White
Editorial Coordinator: Marike van der Veen
Editorial Assistant: Mary M. Saxton

Original English translation by International Editorial Services
Inc./C. E. Berry

First printing. Printed in U.S.A.
Published simultaneously in Canada.

Time Life Inc. is a wholly owned subsidiary of
THE TIME INC. BOOK COMPANY.

TIME LIFE is a trademark of Time Warner Inc. U.S.A.

School and library distribution by Time-Life Education,
P.O. Box 85026, Richmond, Virginia 23285-5026.
For subscription information, call 1-800-621-7026.